FEMALE SOLDIERS IN SIERRA LEONE

GENDER AND POLITICAL VIOLENCE SERIES
General Editor: Laura Sjoberg

Muscular Nationalism: Gender, War, and Empire in India and Ireland, 1914–2004
Sikata Banerjee

Female Soldiers in Sierra Leone: Sex, Security, and Post-Conflict Development
Megan H. MacKenzie

Female Soldiers in Sierra Leone

Sex, Security, and Post-Conflict Development

Megan H. MacKenzie

NEW YORK UNIVERSITY PRESS
New York and London

NEW YORK UNIVERSITY PRESS
New York and London
www.nyupress.org

© 2012 by New York University
All rights reserved

Library of Congress Cataloging-in-Publication Data
MacKenzie, Megan H. (Megan Hazel)
 Female soldiers in Sierra Leone : sex, security, and post-conflict development / Megan H. MacKenzie.
  p. cm. — (Gender and political violence series)
 Includes bibliographical references and index.
 ISBN 978-0-8147-6137-3 (cl : alk. paper)
 ISBN 978-0-8147-7125-9 (ebook)
 ISBN 978-0-8147-4197-0 (ebook)
 1. Women soldiers—Sierra Leone. 2. Sex role—Sierra Leone. 3. Postwar reconstruction—Sierra Leone. 4. Rape as a weapon of war—Sierra Leone. 5. Sierra Leone—History—Civil War, 1991-2002—Participation, Female. 6. Sierra Leone—History—Civil War, 1991-2002—Women. I. Title. II. Series: Gender and political violence series.
 UB419.S5M33 2012
 305.43355009664—dc23
                          2012009364

References to Internet websites (URLs) were accurate at the time of writing.
Neither the author nor New York University Press is responsible
for URLs that may have expired or changed since the manuscript was prepared.

New York University Press books are printed on acid-free paper,
and their binding materials are chosen for strength and durability.
We strive to use environmentally responsible suppliers and materials
to the greatest extent possible in publishing our books.

Manufactured in the United States of America
10 9 8 7 6 5 4 3 2 1

For my mom

CONTENTS

Acknowledgments ix
Foreword: The New Feminist International Relations xi
  Christine Sylvester

1. Introduction: Conjugal Order and Insecurity Post-Conflict 1
2. The History of Sex, Order, and Conflict in Sierra Leone 23
3. Defining Soldiers 45
4. Empowerment Boom or Bust? Assessing Women's Post–Armed Conflict Empowerment Initiatives 63
5. Securitization and Desecuritization: Female Soldiers and the Reconstruction of Women 85
6. Securitizing Sex? Rethinking Wartime Sexual Violence 99
7. Loving Your Enemy: Rape, Sex, Childbirth, and Politics Post–Armed Conflict 117
8. Conclusion: Displacing War Mythology and Developmental Logic 137
   Notes 147
   Index 169
   About the Author 175

ACKNOWLEDGMENTS

The subject matter of much of this book has been emotionally challenging for me— overwhelming at times. If it were not for the encouragement, support, inspiration, and tough love of many people, I suspect this research would have been abandoned in its infancy.

This project was initiated because I developed a feminist curiosity sparked by excellent feminist scholars who were asking important questions. This book is possible because intellectuals like Christine Sylvester, Cynthia Enloe, Carol Cohn, Ann Tickner, Teresia Teaiwa and Lene Hansen carved out space for feminist research within the discipline. I have benefited greatly from the mentorship and encouragement of these scholars, as well as the community and support of the incredible "next generation" of feminists, including Swati Parashar, Annick Wibben, Cristina Masters, and Sungju Park-Kang (among—thankfully!—many more). I especially wish to thank Christine Sylvester for her early encouragement and her continued insightful professional and intellectual advice, as well as Swati Parashar for sharing this journey with trust and understanding—we make a great team.

This book was also possible thanks to numerous people in Sierra Leone who showed me that almost everything I had previously learned about war and its aftermath was irrelevant. Most important were the women who took time from selling groundnuts, attending sewing class, taking care of their children, and the other many necessary tasks that filled their days to answer my questions and share their stories. My commitment to them to write about matters that have impacted their lives, are important to them, and have shaped their post-conflict futures drove this research project and shaped this book. A special thank-you also goes to Father Joseph Momoh, Edward Abu, Dehunge Shiaka, Father Joseph Turay, and Isha Kamara. I am grateful to Liz Oscroft for her endless generosity and wisdom, and for holding my hand through my own reintegration back to Canada after my field research.

When I was at the University of Alberta, Malinda Smith, Lois Harder, and Rob Aitken—encouraged me to stick with a research project that seemed beyond my capabilities and guided me with compassion and grace. I am also thankful for the institutional and intellectual support of both the Women and Public Policy Program and the Belfer Center for Science and International Affairs at Harvard.

I am very grateful for Laura Sjoberg's enthusiasm for this project and for guiding me through the final phases of the book. Thank you also to Morgan Hanks, Marianne Bevan, Dehunge Shiaka, and Mohamed Sesay (and all others), who read early drafts and gave excellent feedback. Gratitude is extended to Robbie Shilliam and Pat Moloney for their advice and friendship. Special thanks to Teresia Teaiwa for her mentorship and for joining me for hours of writing and cookies at Clark's Café in Wellington.

Thank you to my friends and to my family for accepting me and my often depressing topics of conversation. Two of the strongest women I know, my mom and my sister, have been constant sources of support, practical words, and love. Finally, I cannot find words enough to thank my partner in life, Jason, for making me believe that intelligence is beautiful and for inspiring me with his own brilliance and creativity. Together, this life is a joyful adventure.

FOREWORD

The New Feminist International Relations

CHRISTINE SYLVESTER

At last, students of feminist international relations (IR) have become interested in the women hiding in plain view: the women of war and conflict, which is to say the women who become agents of collective violence and, when possible, of post-conflict strategies. The violent woman of international relations is not only more "OK" to study than she once was; she is apt to be visited in situ by academics from a field that used to associate fieldwork with comparative politics, anthropology, and area studies. True IR scholars once seemed to theorize from their university offices and to produce high abstractions as a result. Everyday people were either invisible in international relations, because they were beside the point, or slotted into a few categories of relevance—soldiers, civilians, deaths. Now, along with exposing the many locations once blotted out by a Great Powers focus, analysts of feminist international relations are increasingly going to ground and endeavoring to study up rather than do IR theory at the top. Many are talking to people who have experienced war and conflict and also know personally and politically about post-conflict programs pursued by local and international communities.

Megan MacKenzie is a headliner in this new approach to studying and doing IR. Her book dashes prominent assumptions that war is about states, weapons, and strategies or is, at base, a set of activities that men plan and execute and women mostly suffer and protest. Unless we know women's experiences with one of the most persistent social institutions known to humans—war—all the studies in the world will not be able to overcome fundamental shortcomings around what war is, who and what it involves, and what its consequences are for people and societies. Pressing questions need to be addressed, as they are here, concerning gender-based violence in war and postwar, what "normal" security for women means in different places (e.g., is it conjugal security?), and how the interested researcher can talk to women combatants, hear them, and interpret experiences that are bound to be very distant from her personal and political frames of reference. MacKenzie addresses these and other key issues in the context of a war that took her to Sierra Leone.

She also addresses the much-vaunted concept of post-conflict reconstruction and reconciliation. Exactly who and which norms and institutions are reconstructed in what directions? Does peace after war entail reassigning women to domestic spaces and limited forms of agency? Who reconciles with whom? What is the range of politics that women and girls experience and seek to achieve in situations of war and postwar? And, is their politics acknowledged and facilitated by academicians and by practitioners of development and guardians of human rights on the ground, or is it bypassed in scripts that define security and development from the top rather than up from people's wishes to agencies with resources?

It is a privilege to know some of the leading "new generation" scholars of feminist IR across the world and to hear their war and postwar stories, their new theorizing, and their research anxieties, firsthand and via Skype. When exhausting and trying fieldwork joins up with theory as well as it does in this book by Megan MacKenzie, I know that feminist IR is alive, well, and dwelling everywhere now, not just in some gendered places.

1

Introduction

Conjugal Order and Insecurity Post-Conflict

One of the most illustrative signifiers of Sierra Leone's eleven-year civil conflict is an image of a boy, about twelve years old, wearing tattered clothing and a tough expression and holding an AK-47.[1] Variations of this image have been used on countless pamphlets and posters to "raise awareness" about child soldiers, to solicit donations for war-torn African countries, and to advertise the need for research in the areas of peace and post-conflict. This singular image is used to represent "Africa," or some idea of Africa as a landmass united by troubled civil wars, corruption, and underdevelopment.[2] The young boy soldier symbolizes uncomplicated perceptions of "the African" subject. He embodies the constant possibility of chaos in Africa and the perceived need for outside intervention. Likewise, the boy signifies the lost innocence of childhood specifically and of "traditional" Africa more generally. As a child, he evokes the sense that, though his innocence has been corrupted, there remains a possibility for it to be returned. This feeds the perception of "the tragedy of Africa" and the notion that despite the destruction and losses, it is possible—and the West's "responsibility"—to restore order and peace to this troubled continent.

This boy has become representative of a wider collection of archetypal identities associated with the continent, including the disenfranchised youth, the impoverished citizen, and the uneducated child. When I traveled to Sierra Leone in October 2005, it was clear that this characterization had masked, and somehow eclipsed, other identities. Of these unexplored identities, female soldiers are perhaps one of the most underrepresented categories of "war-affected" citizens. The "official" story of the conflict, reflected in the literature, media accounts, and international nongovernmental organization (INGO) and nongovernmental organization (NGO) reports, largely omits the participation of female soldiers. Furthermore, mainstream narratives recounting the so-called postwar period and the end of armed conflict are reliably mute on the experiences of women and girls. Narratives tend to focus on violent men being disarmed so that society can "return to normal" or can return from anarchy to domesticated order. The chaos and lawlessness that characterized the war period is described as gradually being replaced by peace and structure through the help of development agencies and government intervention. Families reunite, children return to school, and men find new jobs to support their loved ones.

These depictions of conflict and peace in Sierra Leone stood in stark contrast to the narratives of the individuals I interviewed in the country. Local social and aid workers, government officials, volunteers, and leaders of women's organizations uncovered alternative versions of the war and of the post–armed conflict period; these consistently featured female soldiers. Female soldiers dislocate predictable and simplistic gendered representations of war: they displace the typical characterization of an "African rebel" as well as perceptions about disempowered and victimized African women. The disparate accounts of women's and girls' participation in the civil conflict in Sierra Leone evoked several questions: Why, if women participated as soldiers, were they largely ignored in mainstream accounts of the conflict? What where were their stories? How might female soldiers' depictions of the war and accounts of the postwar period enhance and alter mainstream accounts of Sierra Leone's civil war? And how might the recognition of female soldiers disrupt the often singular and generalized depictions of conflict in Africa and complicate the use of a young boy with an AK-47 as the symbol of its wars?

In an effort to shed light on these curiosities, it seemed logical to go straight to the source. Through the assistance of several individuals and organizations I was able to conduct interviews with more than seventy-five female soldiers from across the country. The stories, dreams, complaints, and desires recounted by these women challenge prevailing assumptions associated with development, gender and conflict, violent women, and soldiering. A vast gap soon emerged between existing representations of female soldiers and their own accounts of the conflict and their post–armed conflict situations. The female soldiers interviewed made it clear that the depiction of "women and children" as a coherent category of war victims is overly simplistic and ignores the variety of roles women and girls possess during war as well as their agency during this period. Further, their stories problematized the notion of "post-conflict" as a seamless move from war to peace. Finally, these interviews complicate two particular simplistic generalizations about African civil wars, including the presumption that civil wars are initiated by idle young men who commit random violence and contribute to generalized chaos; second, that women and girls are impacted by, or protected from, war but rarely contribute to, or impact, war themselves.

This book is premised on the belief that stories of war and peace are nothing but gendered myths if they ignore, silence, or exclude women and girls. Without asking about and listening to the experiences of women and girls as well as men and boys during war, we are left with a limited understanding of war, who is involved, what it means to people, and how they are affected in the short and long term. Current understandings of post-conflict, peace, and reintegration in Sierra Leone are equally gendered, due, in part, to an absence of female soldiers' own accounts of the war and the "postwar" period. Without recognizing the roles and experiences of female soldiers in Sierra Leone, post-conflict reconstruction policies are bound to be gender blind at best, and restrictive, moralizing, and disciplining at worst.

Drawing largely from interview material, one of the central aims of this book is to show post-conflict reconstruction as a highly gendered process defined and imposed largely from the outside of so-called war-torn communities. Within much of the literature focused on post–armed conflict states, the processes of post-conflict reconstruction and peace building are presupposed to be benign, inclusive, and progressive. The post-conflict period is often defined as a temporary period after a formal cease-fire characterized by increased peace, possibility, and development. Post-conflict organizations and institutions are seen as neutral actors whose roles are to facilitate the transition from insecurity and conflict to peace and social order. Post-conflict policies are largely shaped by patriarchal norms associated with liberal social order rather than by "local" needs, realities, or particularities. Crowding out space for its critique, this idealized imaginary of the post-conflict phase casts external actors as necessary saviors and obviates questions about the kinds of conflicts and insecurities that might continue after formal cease-fire agreements.

Interviews with female soldiers also inspired the conclusion that key concepts connected with both war and peace, such as order, disorder, security, and insecurity, are gendered and largely assume particular gendered orders. Reconstruction, the return to normal, the restoration of order, and reintegration—the central objectives of most post-conflict policies—are not gender neutral but rather assume and require a particular gendered order. As a result, post-conflict policies have the potential to inscribe and enforce exploitative and patriarchal forms of gendered order post–armed conflict.

Specifically, I argue that notions of conjugal order[3] shape understandings of security and insecurity and are at the heart of development and post–armed conflict reconstruction policies. The concept of conjugal order refers to the laws and social norms that serve to regulate sexuality, (re)construct the family, and send messages about acceptable and legitimate social relationships. There is no singular form of conjugal order; rather, conjugal order can be used as an analytical tool to detect and examine the laws, regulations, and norms that dominate a particular region or context. Conjugal order is informed by the laws associated with marriage and the family, including marital, paternity, adoption, and inheritance laws as well as broader social norms. For most patriarchal societies these norms include the privileging of heterosexual sex, the assumption that sex within marriage is consensual, and customs dictating legitimate and illegitimate children. Conjugal order is inspired by previous work on the regulation of sexuality. What distinguishes this concept from other theoretical analyses of the family and sexuality is that conjugal order is used specifically to understand the links between sexual regulation and broader notions of order and stability. One of the main contentions of this book is that conjugal order shapes perceptions about security and development and that policies aimed at improving security and development impose, institute, and reinforce particular forms of conjugal order.

Periods of insecurity, such as war, are a privileged time for examining how peace, order, and security are defined. Moreover, the phase of transition between war and the so-called postwar period provides a unique opportunity to examine how social order is literally reconstructed through intervening actors, particularly international organizations and NGOs. Female soldiers in Sierra Leone are an exemplary focus because they represent a problem for most iterations of conjugal order: many of these women achieved positions of power unavailable to them outside of conflict, scores were unmarried or involved in unauthorized relationships, most were separated from their parents or family units, and countless had children as a result of rape or as a result of an "illegitimate" relationship. The ways in which the government and local and international actors described, depicted, categorized, and reconstructed these women and girls reveal a great deal about how Western-liberal forms of conjugal order were reconstructed and imposed in Sierra Leone.

In turn, the concept of conjugal order helps unpack not only the gendered nature of development but also the imperial and regulatory nature of development. Policies that assume particular relationships between mothers and fathers, husbands and wives will be shown to be constructing the liberal family model rather than responding to it. Further, the way "legitimate" beneficiaries of development aid are recognized within post-conflict and development policies serves to construct identities and delineate "normal" relationships and behaviors. Policy makers are neither catering their post–armed conflict responses to "local realities" nor restoring local, "natural" order; rather, most post-conflict development policies impose Western-liberal ideals of conjugal order, which send explicitly moralizing messages to individuals about appropriate identities, behaviors, relationships, and values.

Recasting Post-Conflict Development and Security

Post-conflict development continues to be a major global focus for both policy makers and academics. Further, given the growing conflation of security and development, or the "radicalization of development," Western nations are increasingly considering international development as directly impacting their own prosperity and security.[4] As a result, many Western donor governments and Western-based organizations and institutions have taken an active role in overseeing the process of post–armed conflict reconstruction and development. Despite the increased role of international actors in developing nations' affairs—particularly of INGOs and a plethora of development agencies—there has been insufficient critical investigation of the political and ethical rationalities, the endemic gender biases, and the impacts of these actors on developing nations.

Given the tendency of international organizations and development organizations to create and reuse "models"[5] for development projects, investigating and critiquing these models—specifically how women are "processed" through and envisioned by them—is essential. In particular, in a highly securitized moment such as the so-called transition from war to peace, the gendered ordering that takes place in the name of "reconstruction" and "rehabilitation" must be explored. Moreover, identifying the ways in which the "post-conflict" transition in Sierra Leone has been gendered might allow us to locate important sites of resistance and possibilities for change.

This book draws from and contributes to scholarship within the fields of security, development, and gender studies. The work of Mark Duffield and his approach to humanitarianism, development, and post-conflict reconstruction have been particularly inspiring.[6] In *Global Governance and the New Wars*, Duffield coined the phrase "the radicalization of development," in reference to what he sees as the merging of development and security. Duffield argues that, as a result of the radicalization of development, those in the business of development are no longer simply securing the post-conflict environment; their recent mandates include transforming entire societies through the inculcation of "liberal peace."[7] Duffield explains that the coupling of "liberal" and "peace" has meant that liberal policies and structures are correlated with stability: "Liberal values and institutions have been vested with ameliorative and harmonizing powers."[8]

One consequence of this forced marriage between "liberal" and "peace" has been that aid not only is aimed at emergency relief but also is concerned with "conflict resolution, reconstructing social networks, strengthening civil and representative institutions, and security sector reform in the context of a functioning market economy."[9] In other words, the liberal project of development is about radical societal transformation. This conflation of development and security has pushed aid agencies and NGOs operating development programs from the role of distributors of philanthropic donations to political directors and governors, or, the organizers of society characterized by liberal democracy and liberal political economy. Duffield summarizes this idea: "Aid is no substitute for political action because it is the political action. It is now a tool of international regulation and is embedded in the networks and strategic complexes that make up liberal peace."[10]

This book focuses specifically on the ways in which the radicalization of development has affected ideas about post–armed conflict reconstruction and reintegration. Reconstruction and reintegration tend to be viewed as neutral concepts, which signify a "return to normal" post–armed conflict. There is little research that considers the genealogy of the concept of reintegration and its multiple meanings in post-conflict discourses. The term "reintegration" is rooted within criminology literature; the most basic definition given in criminology is "a process intended to reduce recidivism after a criminal's release from prison."[11] In this context, two facets of reintegration are described. First, reintegration is seen as a process: "Reintegration (or 're-entry' as it is sometimes called) is both an event and a process. . . . re-entry is also a long-term process, one that actually starts prior to release and continues well afterwards."[12] The second dynamic of reintegration is associated with "correction," "rehabilitation," and "treatment" and is aimed at preparing criminals to be successful citizens.[13] What is implied by these definitions is that criminals have deviated from societal norms and must be transformed or molded in such a way as to ensure that they can return to and function "normally" in society.

Within literature looking at the disarmament process, reintegration is defined generally as "the process which allows ex-combatants and their families to adapt economically and socially to productive civilian life."[14] In this sense, reintegration in the "post-conflict" context is conceived in a similar way to reintegration within criminology. Both assume a desistance of criminal or combat behavior, "reentry" into community or civilian life, and rehabilitation or an adaptation of behavior to discourage recidivism. When reviewing the reintegration policies associated with Sierra Leone's disarmament process, these similarities become clear. For example, the National Committee for Disarmament, Demobilization and Reintegration (NCDDR) declared that reintegration policies were designed to support *"resettlement into normal* society."[15]

There is a growing body of research that examines the gendered power dynamics associated with reintegration, as well as "post-conflict" in general. Susan McKay and Dyan Mazurana's text *Where Are the Girls? Girls in Fighting Forces in Northern Uganda, Sierra Leone, and Mozambique: Their Lives during and after War,* is a well-known example of a gendered analysis of reintegration programs.[16] This literature has shown that while women typically take on different roles during conflict, this does not necessarily translate into power and authority in their communities post–armed conflict.[17] Mary Caprioli explains that "the national patriarchy begins to reassert itself after the war and expects women to return to 'the way they were before the war'" or "to their subordinate positions."[18] McKay similarly concludes, "The [post-conflict] reality usually proves that, regardless of culture and place, women's roles revert to traditional ones, and nationalistic loyalties are more highly valued than is gender equality."[19]

The Copenhagen school's approach to security fits well with Duffield's analysis of the radicalization of development and is referred to throughout the book. According to the Copenhagen school, security is not a fixed concept and cannot be defined in a static manner. Instead, it is argued that security is constructed through the "speech act," or the act of securitizing actors naming and thereby constructing a security concern. Securitizing actors are defined as individuals, or a group—including government, leaders, or military groups—who perform the speech act.[20] Once a matter has been securitized, it is prioritized above "normal politics," and "extraordinary means" are necessary to address the problem.[21] As a result of this prioritization, Rita Abrahamsen argues that securitization "has clear political implications."[22] These implications result from the heightened profile and increased attention typically given to securitized issues in terms of policy making, funding, and media attention.

The Copenhagen school's rendering of securitization as a speech act places the securitizing actor and the audience as the central players in the construction of security. According to this approach, parties who are able to constitute a security concern typically hold positions of power and possess a "particular legitimacy."[23] Securitization then becomes a strategic practice aimed at swaying a targeted audience to accept the securitizing actor's interpretation of a threat. In this way, securitization is an intersubjective process in the sense that it is only when the audience accepts a securitizing actor's speech act that an issue will become securitized.

My work is indebted to Duffield and the Copenhagen school and other critical scholarship that challenges traditional notions of development and security; however, there remain some essential questions about gender and sexuality in relation to development and security that cannot be analyzed effectively within these approaches. There has been insufficient analysis of the gendered implications of the radicalization of development, or the merging of development and security. The central obstacle or deficiency is that most approaches to security have been overly transfixed with "security flashes," or issues deemed an immediate public security matter. Realists use the terms "high" politics and "low" politics, while the Copenhagen school uses "normal" politics and "securitized" matters, but the heart of the matter is that none of these approaches consider the significance of the so-called domestic sphere in shaping our understanding of security. Concentrating only on "security flashes" obscures the broader social context within which security matters are shaped and discounts the possibility that "security" always already depends on the construction and reconstruction of normal, domestic, and peaceful politics.

As a feminist scholar, I am particularly interested in how the radicalization of development might result in policies that give primacy to those development issues deemed a public security concern. In contrast, those issues deemed "private" or "domestic" concerns will be deprioritized and obscured by this attention to the "security flashes." Although gender often remains an afterthought or a side note to so-called harder international relations issues, the literature on gender and war is diverse and growing significantly.[24] The dominant understanding of women as victims in war is evident in literature that constructs women as "naturally" peaceful and men as naturally violent and aggressive.

I build on the feminist work that has concluded that "post-conflict," "peace," and "rehabilitation" are misnomers for women because they presume the benefits of "going back," or "restoring to a position or capacity that previously existed," without sufficiently considering the oppressive or violent nature of the previous power arrangements and institutions.[25] Critical research has done much to disrupt dominant conceptions of the post-conflict moment as a universally positive transition from war to peace; however, there is still much to be done in terms of investigating the gendered nature of post-conflict policies, the biases of international organizations in relation to gendered roles and needs post–armed conflict, the gendered nature of conflict resolution processes, the power arrangements that take place post–armed conflict, and the actors involved in facilitating and instituting power arrangements.

Moreover, while there is certainly evidence that women, children, and the elderly are vulnerable during war, that they are more likely to be uprooted due to conflict and are more likely to experience sexual violence, there is also important research by scholars such as Cynthia Enloe, Charli Carpenter, Elise Barth, Louise Olsson, Inger Skjelsbaek, Karen Hostens, Patricia T. Morris, and Tina Johnson that demands a reconsideration of broad gendered generalizations about victims and perpetrators in war. Rather than focusing on the impact of war *on* women, feminist international relations scholars such as Christine Sylvester, Swati Parashar, Myriam Denov, Laura Sjoberg, and Caron Gentry have recounted the historical contributions of women *to* warfare.[26] In particular, there is a burgeoning literature on female soldiers and female militants, with a particular surge in scholarship examining women's participation in terrorist activities after 9/11.[27] Despite the increased attention to women's participation in conflict, there remain few academic resources looking at female soldiers in the context of African civil conflicts. Many of the available resources are reports from organizations like the Canadian International Development Agency (CIDA),[28] United Nations country reports or research documents,[29] or research institute reports.[30] Among the few resources focusing specifically on female soldiers in Sierra Leone, the majority concentrate on girl soldiers.[31]

Like that of Christine Sylvester, my work draws from both critical feminist and postcolonial literature.[32] Postcolonialism here does not refer to the "end" of colonialism; rather, it speaks to the continuations and legacies of colonialism. Dominated by Edward Said's notion of Orientalism, or the production and reproduction of the "Orient" in relation to "the Occident," which has historically described the West as superior,[33] postcolonial studies is particularly concerned with identifying and locating sites of resistance against the ways in which the third world is represented by, and constructed through, hegemonic Western discourses.

This focus on the constructions of the West and "the rest" has inspired those in postcolonial and subaltern studies to reflect on the significance of self-representation. In "Can the Subaltern Speak?"[34] Gayatri Chakravorty

Spivak asks if third world women have the agency required to express themselves given their subordinate positions of power. She warns that even when third world women speak, their voices are restricted by the limits and avenues allotted to them; their voices are always mediated and therefore controlled by others: "Between patriarch and imperialism, subject-constitution and object-formation, the figure of the woman disappears."[35] However, she urges the postcolonial critic to take account of these silences and find ways to break the dominance of imperial and patriarchal hegemonic ideas. The emphasis on voice, representation, and agency demanded by both feminist and postcolonial theory serves as a linchpin for my own theoretical and methodological approach.

Each chapter in this volume places significant emphasis on the voices of the women and men interviewed in Sierra Leone. These interviews, and the voices they represent, act as disruptions to dominant discourses associated with gendered norms, power, conflict, and development. In taking Spivak's warning, I neither pretend to offer the interviews as "truth" nor ignore my role in constructing this book and the potential for misinterpretation and misrepresentation.

Reconstructing Conjugal Order

My own theoretical approach centers on the concept of conjugal order and is founded on the assumption that gender is at the center of ideas of security and development. The "order" that is implicit to notions of peace and stability depends on multiple gender constructions. Periods of insecurity, such as war, are a privileged time for examining how peace, order, and security are defined. Most of the literature on war focuses on atrocities, war crimes, foreign policy and strategy, or the public events and activities of war—or the "security flashes." I argue these events can only be defined and understood through their distinction from orderly, peaceful, and "normal" society. In other words, it is impossible to understand security events without some understanding of order and normality. Of particular significance is "the domestic" to these ideas of order, peace, and "normal."

As already mentioned, conjugal order refers not only to the institution of marriage but also to the laws and broader social norms associated with marriage and the family, including the privileging of heterosexual sex and the assumption that sex within marriage is consensual. This notion of conjugal order draws on Michel Foucault's work on sexual regulation; Jacques Donzelot's thought on the family and philanthropy; Jacqueline Stevens's work on the nuclear family, laws, and gender subordination; and Lene Hansen's approach to identity formation. Foucault identifies the deployment of sexuality and the surveillance of sex and the body as one of the most significant technologies of power.[36] He demonstrates how the linking of sexuality to sex allows for the artificial grouping of elements such as "health, progeny, race, the future of the species, the vitality of the social body" with "anatomical elements, biological functions, conducts, sensations, and pleasures."[37] This linking indicates how the regulation of sex acts as a sort of linchpin that served to fuel capitalist economic growth, manufacture legitimacy, and "normalize" behavior.

Like other disciplinary mechanisms, those directed at regulating sexuality take both an explicit judicial form and an implicit "normalizing" form. At the center of the history of sexuality and the disciplining of sexuality is the family model. Most of the "economic and political problems" associated with population, including birth rate, age of marriage, legitimate and illegitimate births, sexual relations, fertility or sterility, and the effects of the unmarried could be controlled through the institution of the family unit.[38] Foucault—like Jacqueline Stevens—notes the significance of the "husband wife axis" and the "parents children axis" in the deployment of sexuality.[39] The "normalization" of these relationships through the creation and surveillance of the family represents one of the most significant yet largely unexamined forms of sexual regulation. As Foucault noted, the "family was the crystallization in the deployment of sexuality: [it] seemed to be the source of sexuality which it actually only reflected and diffracted."[40] In other words, while the family appears to be a natural formation, it is in fact the product of a highly advanced set of regulatory mechanisms.

Donzelot applies Foucault's work on discipline and sexuality to the liberal state. Donzelot argues that the family is an "anchorage point for private property and its function of reproduction of the ruling ideology."[41] Due to the surveillance and governance opportunities offered through the working-class family model, it is defined by Donzelot as the smallest political organization possible. In turn, not belonging to a family is seen as a social problem and a source of potential instability and threat.

Donzelot's work on philanthropy and the change in attitudes regarding tutelage provides a strong footing from which to rethink the significance of the family and conjugal order as well as the role of development actors in constructing gender. In *The Policing of Families*, Donzelot notes how the family became central to changes in eighteenth-century philanthropy. He argues that open donations were replaced with targeted aid aimed at "saving" citizens from the potential of becoming vagabonds and beggars.[42] The nuclear family unit was at the heart of this targeted aid and was seen as a vehicle through which delinquent individuals could be absorbed "while at the same time it becomes an agent for conveying the norms of the state into the private sphere."[43]

The transformations within philanthropy Donzelot identifies mirror current trends within international development. Rather than generalized responses to poverty and crisis, development—through measures such as tied aid and targeted aid—has increasingly exhibited specific social and moral objectives, including (re)establishing liberal social order, encouraging the establishment of liberal democratic values, and the stabilization and liberalization of the economy. Recently, "new humanitarianism" has been used to refer to the process whereby generalized, neutral development assistance is replaced with targeted, "politically conscious" aid aimed at societal transformation and governance.[44] New humanitarianism is presented as a novel approach to development capable of addressing the past failures of development initiatives through these types of targeted initiatives.

Both new humanitarianism and Donzelot's philanthropy represent a shift from benevolent donations to a process of direct investment in society—with expected return. In both conceptualizations, the return on the investment is said to be guaranteed through the restrictions and regulations placed on the funding. In other words, conditions are placed on the funding to ensure it is used in specific ways and that it will produce specific outcomes. In both cases, the rules, norms, and regulations placed on donations act as forms of social and economic regulation. Gilles Deleuze summarizes the impact of such targeted philanthropy, "The social comes into being with a system . . . in which norms replace the law, regulatory and corrective mechanisms replace the standard."[45] Fiona Fox explains the effects of new humanitarianism: "Conditional humanitarian aid is becoming yet another tool available to Western governments to control developing countries."[46]

Neither Foucault nor Donzelot takes his analysis of the family further and considers gender subordination or the impacts of the way in which notions of the family privilege certain gendered identities and relationships while obscuring or rendering problematic others. Jacqueline Stevens helps push this discussion forward with her analysis of the so-called natural family unit, arguing that paternity and marriage laws serve both to control reproduction and to give power to husbands and fathers. Stevens identifies three ways in which marriage bestows males with significant power and rights over women and children. First, a woman's nationality or citizenship is partly determined by her husband's. Second, males have political rights to children produced by their wives. Third, the name and nationality of children in most societies are bestowed through husbands. Stevens is adamant that the access and power that men gain through women formalize relationships of gender inequality:

> Rather than pre-existing sex differences being reflected in and exacerbated by laws, the very definition of matrimony suggests the institution is constitutive of inequity in roles related to reproduction, that marriage is an asymmetrical system assuring men access to mothers (mater), creating unrecognized and largely unrequited demands on women.[47]

Stevens is arguing that through the regulation of marriage and birth the state constructs women as natural and prepolitical and men as "heads" of households, or the natural "breadwinners." She concludes that women are relegated to the private sphere of child rearing and domestic work while men are situated in the political realm as administrators of the family unit.

Stevens also argues that what is considered "natural" is in fact constructed and regulated, in part, through the disciplinary tactics of the state. Stevens adds that the result of normalizing or naturalizing "is to express the necessity of a form of being or practice, to make something seem impervious to human intention and immutable."[48] It follows that by rendering the family as a "natural" unit, it is also defined as necessary, unchanging, and outside the realm of political intervention. This logic has helped to produce and justify the distinction between the political (public) and "private" realms. In addition, this logic legitimates noninterventionist approaches to issues deemed "domestic" concerns.[49]

Lene Hansen's work on identity formation is also helpful here. She has identified two ways in which policies can erase particular gendered identities. She argues that policies not only construct particular identities but also exclude or delegitimize other identities. In a securitized arena, it is often gendered identities that are left out or rendered "illegitimate." Second, the intersubjective nature of security policies assumes that subjects are able to voice their concerns. Hansen uses the examples of female victims of bride burnings in Pakistan to illustrate her point that not all citizens—particularly those who fall in the category of "illegitimate identity"—can participate in an equal exchange; therefore, they are excluded from the public realm of policy making and politics.

The ordering that Foucault, Donzelot, Stevens, and Hansen refer to in relation to the regulation of sex informs the concept of conjugal order used throughout this book. The book is primarily focused on the international response to the civil war in Sierra Leone and, in particular, the disarmament, demobilization, and reintegration process that was driven by international donors. As a result, attention is paid to how conjugal order is implied and constructed through international policies and programs.[50] What distinguishes the concept of conjugal order from other work on sexual regulation and identity formation is that the concept is not simply useful in an analysis of sexual regulation; rather, it can be employed to scrutinize the gendered biases endemic to understandings of development and security. It is important to take note of sexual regulation, but also to look beyond the process of regulating sex to see how ideas about conjugal order inform and dictate our perceptions about order, peace, security, and development more broadly. Many general development "problems" are actually problems associated with conjugal *dis*order, including female-headed households, family planning, orphans, unaccompanied children, and "idle" men. In turn, I make the following conclusion about the reciprocal relationship between conjugal order and notions of security and development: conjugal order is foundational to the meanings of development and security; development policies—particularly those driven by concerns with insecurity—impose and institute a largely Western-liberal conjugal order.

The conflation of security and development priorities associated with the radicalization of development closes off space for reflection on and critique of the gendered nature of development priorities and policies. Sources of insecurity become the focus while order is taken as a given. Development policies serve to reconstruct communities and reintegrate individuals according to a particular Western-liberal notion of "normal" society. Western-liberal notions of conjugal order are at the heart of notions of normality, peace, order, and security. As a result, especially as development becomes securitized, post-conflict development policies act as forms of discipline or regulation. Post-conflict policies discipline individuals by sending explicit messages about "normal" and legitimate behaviors and roles. In addition, these policies serve both to construct acceptable and normalized gendered subjects and to reinforce and construct gendered power dynamics.

Chapter Overview

Most policies aimed at restoring peace and promoting development in Sierra Leone depended on specific notions of conjugal order. Focusing on the reintegration process for female soldiers, each chapter in this book considers the significance of conjugal order to notions of peace, stability, and normality.

Chapter 2 looks at the history of sexual regulation in Sierra Leone and how British colonizers took care to regulate everything from sex with prostitutes to adoption practices. This chapter is not meant as a comprehensive overview of Sierra Leone's history; rather, it should highlight for the reader the sociopolitical context of gender ordering and sexual regulation in Sierra Leone. Specifically, this chapter provides readers with the historical and political background necessary for understanding current post-conflict policies and power relations. It includes an analysis of historical continuities and discontinuities—particularly in relation to sexual governance, family structures and law, and the status of women and girls in Sierra Leone.

Chapter 3 presents a critical examination of the way "soldier" and "victim" identities are constructed and reconstructed by "post-conflict" programs in Sierra Leone. It is argued that characterizations of women post–armed conflict are largely based on gender stereotypes and specific iterations of conjugal order. This chapter also considers the reluctance of reintegration agencies to identify females who participated in war as soldiers. In addition to the process of categorization, this chapter considers the gap between representations of females both during and after the conflict and the personal narratives of these women. It is argued that by giving female soldiers titles such as "females associated with the war," "dependents," or "camp followers," dominant discourses depoliticize and "naturalize" women's roles during the conflict.

In much the same way that Uma Kothari talks about "the tyranny of participation," chapter 4 examines some of the contradictions associated with the concept of empowerment. It considers how various agencies and organizations such as the World Bank, the United Nations, and NGOs have incorporated empowerment into their programs directed toward women. Focusing on reintegration programs for female soldiers as a case study, this chapter investigates the ways in which empowerment is used by development and aid agencies and organizations and the genealogy of this concept within these discourses. The dominance of neoliberal ideals within so-called empowerment initiatives is demonstrated. This supports the contention that empowerment projects—including the reintegration process in Sierra Leone—are informed by liberal understandings of conjugal order and serve to discipline subjects with explicit messages about appropriate gendered social order and legitimate behaviors.

Chapter 5 examines how the ideal of the female war victim has impacted how former female combatants have been "processed" through disarmament and reintegration programs. It is asserted that men and masculinity are securitized post–armed conflict while women are "desecuritized" and, in effect, de-emphasized in post–armed conflict policy making. Focusing on the absence of individual testimonies and interviews with female soldiers, uniform perceptions of women and girls as victims, "left behind" in a male-dominated war, are questioned. As in the other core chapters of this book, interviews with female soldiers are contrasted to mainstream characterizations of women. The focus in this chapter is on women's explanations of why they did not participate in the disarmament process. The diverse, complex, rational, and emotional responses to this question stand in stark contrast to the sterilized and oversimplified reports of women and girls being "left behind" or "forgotten" by the disarmament, demobilization, and reintegration (DDR) process.

In chapter 6, I propose that sexual violence within Sierra Leone and in other conflict settings across the world is a useful tool of war because it disrupts conjugal order. As a result of conjugal order, men are ordained with power, rights, and access to the labor of women. In turn, the act of rape not only impacts the victim but also creates broader disorder because it violates accepted norms and infringes on the "property" assured to men within a particular community. This reiterates the argument that security flashes are created and understood as a result of deeply embedded understandings of conjugal order.

Chapter 7 builds on the analysis of wartime rape offered in chapter 6, with a focus on children born as a result of such rape. Here it is argued that stigmas associated with wartime rape and children born as a result of rape[51] are a result of policies and legal structures that designate the liberal family model as the norm. Through interviews as well as existing literature, the little information that exists about children born of war in Sierra Leone is presented. The exclusion of children born of wartime rape from development and humanitarian agencies' existing categories of vulnerable children (child soldiers, abandoned children, and street children) is strongly critiqued; it is argued that this exclusion is a strategic choice based on the assumption that sex and the family are not political or security issues.

The final chapter draws together some final conclusions about female soldiers in Sierra Leone and reintegration policies and processes. This chapter also highlights broader insights into the imperial and gendered nature of development policies and "models," and the significance of the family and the so-called domestic sphere to international politics and security studies. Finally, the chapter encourages feminist scholars to continue to reenvision and reconceptualize security and development.

Feminist Methodology

Focusing on female soldiers in post–armed conflict Sierra Leone as a case study, the aim of this book is to use conjugal order as a conceptual tool to understand the significance of sex and the family to notions of security and development. There are multiple ways of interpreting conjugal order in Sierra Leone. First, there are differences in practices and customs between the various ethnic groups and tribes in the country. Second, there is a noticeable divide between practices in Freetown and what was once known as the "protectorate," or the rural areas of the country. Third, as a result of British colonial rule, Sierra Leone inherited, and continues to use, many British family laws. Recognizing this complexity, this book concentrates on mapping how outside actors—primarily international organizations and institutions—imposed Western-liberal forms of conjugal order in Sierra Leone following the armed conflict.

Hansen concluded that "to understand language as *political* is to see it as a site for the production and reproduction of particular subjectivities and identities."[52] Stevens also described discourse as "the field where the regulatory norms of sex are observed."[53] Similarly, Michelle Lazar and Judith Butler argue that power is performed through language, and gender and gendered power relations are continually performed through discourses.[54] Lazar claims that "discourse [is] a site of struggle, where forces of social (re)production and contestation are played out."[55] Given the focus on constructions of gender and conjugal order within this book, feminist critical discourse analysis is the most useful methodology. There certainly is no single definition of either discourse or discourse analysis; however, I am sympathetic to Ernesto Laclau and Chantal Mouffe's approach to it. Laclau and Mouffe posit that discourse is constructed through multiple networks, is historically situated, and places severe limits on what can and cannot be articulated.[56] Laclau and Mouffe are perhaps most noted for their effort to abandon strictly defining discourse in relation to text. Instead, they argue that anything which can represent or convey meaning, including text, economic relationships, institutions, and technology, should be considered part of "discourse."[57]

Fueled by the notion that deconstructing or altering hegemonic discourses can result in ideological and moral shifts, feminist discourse analysis is aimed at locating discourses that sustain or construct patriarchy—that is, relationships of subordination or suppression for women—in order to locate spaces for resistance. In this book I apply this understanding of discourse analysis to my examination of multiple sources of discourse, including government reports and laws,[58] NGO and international development agency policy documents and research reports,[59] existing research on female soldiers in Sierra Leone, and first-person interviews with social workers, former disarmament officials, activists, government officials, and former female soldiers.

My interviews with former female soldiers are the central focus of much of the book. To provide the reader with a more complete idea of the methodology, it is important to offer details about the interview process and as much information as possible about the women I interviewed and the context within which they were interviewed. All interviews were conducted in Sierra Leone between October and December 2005. During this time I was fortunate enough to be invited to Makeni, a town near the center of Sierra Leone that was a major rebel stronghold for much of the civil war. As such, as armed fighting drew down, Makeni was a natural choice for the establishment of one of the major disarmament, demobilization, and reintegration centers. By the time I arrived in Makeni in 2005, most of the DDR initiatives had long since ended. The impacts of DDR programming could be seen in the numerous Honda motorcycle taxis buzzing around the town; in this region, one of the primary reintegration training initiatives aimed at providing men with driving skills and access to vehicles as a means of making a living.

One major reintegration program that remained in operation in Makeni was a joint program between the Catholic Church and the United Nations International Children's Emergency Fund (UNICEF), designed to assist former female soldiers and women abducted by armed groups to reintegrate into society. Specifically, the project recognized that most women had not gone through a formal DDR process and was targeted at those women who were "left behind" by the "post-conflict" reintegration process in the country. More than 200 women were enrolled in the program, which provided participants with a year of training in fabric dyeing, weaving, tailoring, soap making, or catering. These women came from all factions of the fighting forces in Sierra Leone, including the Revolutionary United Front, the Sierra Leone Army, the Armed Forces Revolutionary Council, and the Civil Defence Forces (the Kamajors). The program included women of varied ages; however, the majority were between seventeen and thirty years old.

After being introduced to the coordinators of the program, I was given permission to conduct interviews on the campus and encouraged to stay next door at the Catholic seminary. I interviewed fifty women on campus at the training facility. In constructing my interview questions, I had two priorities. First, it was necessary that my questions did not require the interviewees to delve into personal and potentially traumatic information; second I was required to protect the identity of the interviewees. I was also limited to using a set list of questions for which I had attained ethics approval. The limitation of these questions was that they inhibited more informal discussions and my ability to ask for elaboration from women on certain points. I made every effort to keep the interviews "conversation-like" and informal; however, this was not always possible.

In an effort to make interviewees feel comfortable, safe, and secure, interviews with former soldiers were conducted in pairs in the presence of a social worker. I chose to interview the women in pairs because I felt it diminished the formal atmosphere of a one-on-one interview. Local social workers who had worked with the training program and these women supported this decision and suggested that I allow the women to choose their interview partners; in this way, women were interviewed with someone with whom they felt comfortable. In many cases, having two women together made the interview feel more like a group conversation rather than a strict direct question-and-answer format. It also meant that the interviewee was not "outnumbered" by myself and the social worker; rather, the power dynamics were more evenly balanced by having two interviewees in addition to myself and the social worker.

The social worker present in the interviews acted as my translator. All interviewees spoke in either Krio, Mende, or Temne.[60] Krio is a lingua franca spoken across the country, particularly in Freetown, the Peninsula, the Banana Islands, and York Island; Mende is spoken in the south central areas, and Temne in the Northern Province. There were both benefits and disadvantages to having a social workers act as translator. In terms of benefits, the women had already shared details of their experience with the social worker, and so they were not "double disclosing" to myself and another stranger (an official translator). Second, the social worker was able to brief me regarding the appropriateness or sensitivity of my questions. This process was certainly not perfect; however, I have every assurance from the social workers that the final translations are accurate.

The second group of interviewees were all located in the eastern suburbs of Freetown. This part of the capital city was ravaged by rebel forces during a 1999 invasion infamously called "Operation No Living Thing."[61] At the end of the conflict many former soldiers settled in this area, which remains one of the poorest parts of the city. Interestingly, I gained access to the women in this group through a small organization operating on a shoestring budget and largely driven by one man, Edward Anague. Anague had a piece of land with a couple of very modest buildings, which he used as a center for those affected by the war. Anague saw his center as the place where those who had "slipped through the cracks" could find help. Residents and visitors included amputees, prostitutes, abandoned children, street children, former soldiers, an albino male who had been ostracized from his community, and HIV-positive men, women, and children.

Edward Anague assisted me in conducting the interviews with this cohort of twenty-five former female soldiers. He knew these women through his center and had established a relationship of trust. Most of the interviews were conducted in English or Kriol, with Anague translating the responses into English. One difference between this group of women and the fifty women from Makeni is that these women seemed to be in far more desperate situations. Many of the women were working as prostitutes, some were homeless, and few had any reliable source of income.

There were no other major differences or patterns in the answers from the two groups of women. Both cohorts of female soldiers included women who had served with all major fighting factions; they were from various regions across the country and had participated in the conflict for periods extending from two weeks to ten years. Thus, the total population of former female soldiers interviewed were from diverse backgrounds and gave a broad picture of what life was like for female soldiers during the civil war and in its aftermath.

These interviews provide one of the few representative direct accounts of the roles and experiences of female soldiers in Sierra Leone and represent one of the largest bodies of information from female soldiers in Sierra Leone. Interviews with female soldiers across the global south are relatively rare because they are difficult and/or unsafe to conduct and because there has not been a consistent desire to speak to and learn from these women. The few organizations or researchers that include interviews with female soldiers rarely include high numbers of interviewees.[62] For example, a major report by the Post-Conflict Reintegration Initiative for Development and Empowerment (PRIDE) on ex-combatant views of the Truth and Reconciliation Commission and the Special Court in Sierra Leone draws general conclusions about women's perceptions of the process based only on twenty-one interviews.[63]

All seventy-five of the interviewees were between the ages of eighteen and thirty-two, which means some were child soldiers during the conflict. For a number of reasons, I chose not to separate those women who fought as adults from those who fought as children. First, as I elaborate in chapter 5, the Western definition of a child soldier as someone under the age of eighteen is not representative of Sierra Leonean understandings of "child" and "adult." Moreover, during the course of the eleven-year civil war, many individuals were unsure of their exact age and participated in the war from "childhood" into "adulthood"; therefore, distinguishing their experiences as children from their experiences as adults is not possible or useful. Second, it is not my objective to differentiate between women's and girls' roles and activities during the war; rather, it is to show the broader gender stereotypes and omissions in mainstream depictions of the war and in "post-conflict" policies.

It is important to be clear from the outset that I am not arguing that the two groups of women interviewed are entirely representative of all female soldiers in Sierra Leone. I also acknowledge that this is not an anthropological project. I did not spend extensive time living within communities or conduct any form of participatory observation. I interviewed seventy-five women and more than twenty-five local experts about the reintegration process in Sierra Leone. In the end, I feel confident in the choices I made and recognize the limitations and benefits associated with those choices.

The approach I took in conducting interviews was particularly sensitive to feminist critiques of, and recommendations for, interview techniques. Adler and Worrall summarize the critical feminist argument that women's stories, and the way they are told, can provide the most valuable sources of "evidence" of the structures of power within society and women's and girl's experiences within those structures:

> Violence stories are powerful vehicles conveying information about girls' views and normative beliefs concerning violence. In telling such stories, girls draw on their personal and emotional experiences, and their wider cultural and social life, to convey feelings of both powerlessness and empowerment.... Examining how girls *speak* about violence allows us to trace the multiplicity of ways in which it connects with and impacts upon other areas of their (gendered) lives, and enables us to see the ways in which actual and threatened violence structures daily social interactions.[64]

I include as much of my primary research as possible in the following chapters. Where appropriate, I have incorporated larger sections of interview material to allow the reader to "hear" the voices of the female soldiers and other interviewees. In keeping with this approach, I chose not to edit and disaggregate all the longer quotations into precise thematic topics. Rather than splicing and cutting and pasting each section of quotation to serve the purposes of the chapter, some longer quotations have been left in full and therefore seem less strictly cohesive, including references to multiple themes or weaving together several topics.

In the end, this book represents one of the few analyses of the Sierra Leone conflict that takes gender seriously and places the lives and the stories of women at the forefront. Highlighting women's experiences of Sierra Leone's war and its "post-conflict" reconstruction creates an alternative narrative of these periods and challenges dominant war myths. Shifting the focus to gender and women's experiences of war and peace highlights aspects of the conflict and post–armed conflict period—including wartime rapes, marriage, female perpetrators, training programs for soldiers, "war babies"— that are often either left out or included as minor references in warfare literature. Furthermore, many analyses of the civil war in Sierra Leone—as well as other conflicts—tend to focus exclusively either on the war (as a time of insecurity) or on the post-conflict period (as a time of reconstruction and peace building). This book reveals cracks in this perceived line between "conflict" and "post-conflict" and argues that it is only by listening to, and taking seriously, the experiences of individuals during war and its aftermath that the links between the domestic, "the mundane," the family, sex, and warfare politics can be revealed.

2

The History of Sex, Order, and Conflict in Sierra Leone

If de clause day—O ye big men
O ye men who go to Church;
O ye men who get the money:
O ye men who get the voice;
Stand up—wake up—things day bad, mind
Save de little girls from death
Save de Creole girls from ruin[1]

The majority of the current literature on Sierra Leone tends to focus on one of the following: the "chaotic" nature of Africa in general and West Africa in particular,[2] the eleven-year civil conflict[3], the role of blood diamonds in conflicts,[4] child soldiers,[5] and the lessons to be learned from the United Nations' mission and intervention in the Sierra Leone conflict.[6] There is a dearth of critical scholarship that explores the roles and activity of women during the war or their lives post–armed conflict. Perhaps the most notable omission in this literature is in primary data such as individual interviews—not just with female soldiers but also with local citizens in general. In effect, much of the literature about the Sierra Leone conflict and the post–armed conflict period is not inclusive of voices and perspectives of the country's citizens; rather, the literature is characterized by accounts in which investigators "speak for" the citizens of Sierra Leone. This chapter provides an overview of the historical context of Sierra Leone with a focus on what information is available on gender ordering and sexual regulation. This chapter is not meant to be a comprehensive overview of Sierra Leone's history; rather, it should highlight for the reader the sociopolitical context of gender ordering and sexual regulation in Sierra Leone.

Sierra Leone is situated on the west coast of Africa. It is bordered by beautiful beaches and the Atlantic Ocean to the west, Liberia to the south, and Guinea to the north. With a population of more than 5 million, Sierra Leone has remained at the bottom of the United Nations' Human Development Index for well over a decade. Its struggling economy, with a gross domestic product per capita of approximately $806, is primarily based on the mining of diamonds and minerals as well as small-scale cash crop farming. Despite the gloomy reports for Sierra Leone's economic development, the country has witnessed some major successes in the past few years, including its presidential election in 2007—its second peaceful and democratic presidential election since the end of the civil war.

Long before colonizers set foot in the territory that is now identified as Sierra Leone, assorted ethno-cultural groups, dominated by the Mende, Temne, and Limba, were established in the area. The region was also home to distinctive groups that had migrated from North and East Africa over centuries.[7] Tribes were organized under a chiefdom system whereby a local chief ruled each major region. Most ethnic groups practiced some form of animism while Islam was introduced early to the northern regions of Sierra Leone, and eventually—through colonization—Christianity was brought to the region.

Gender Norms and Ordering
in Sierra Leone

This book is focused on conjugal order and the continuities and discontinuities in current sexual norms and regulations related to gender in Sierra Leone. A look at secret societies can provide some insights into historical and contemporary gender roles in Sierra Leone. Secret societies are organized, all-male or all-female cultural organizations that have existed in West Africa for centuries. Secret societies are organized according to sex rather than ethnicity; the female-only groups are often referred to as Bundu or Sande societies, and the male-only groups are called Poro.[8] These groups initiate members through sacred ceremonies, and members receive education and training particular to their society. Both male and female secret societies focus on teaching their members local history as well as training them in relevant skills for survival and success. Although the details of each society are "secret," it is generally known that male members are taught skills such as hunting, harvesting palm oil, climbing trees, catching animals, and building houses.[9] Female societies train women in skills such as cooking, breast-feeding and child rearing, and running a household.[10] The practices and structures of each society vary according to geography; societies teach their members skills that are relevant to their particular region or period of time. For example, Father Joseph Momoh, a Sierra Leonean priest, explained that some secret society training was "warlike" to teach members how to fight and survive battle because "the community develop[ed] its identity through war."[11] He also reported that some societies teach signs and signals known only to that particular group and that members have used these communication skills to signal to one another on the road or during conflict.[12]

In the past, persons entering adulthood were initiated into secret societies. Most accounts indicate that the average age of initiation into the societies is anywhere from twelve to eighteen; however, because of poverty or the disruption of regular society practices and traditions due to conflict, these ages have fluctuated dramatically over the years. Such secret societies are viewed as a right of passage for the girls and boys of a community; when a child is nearing adulthood, he or she is initiated into one of the local secret societies—usually the same society that his or her parents belong to. The sole definition of adulthood for some communities in Sierra Leone rests on initiation and membership in a secret society. Momoh explains, "If you have a boy of fifteen that goes through a local ceremony to adulthood…and another man of sixty who has not gone through the same ceremony, you treat the fifteen-year-old as a man to be respected and as the elder."[13]

Due to the significance of membership within communities, exclusion from secret societies can be detrimental. Membership not only is required to be considered an adult but also is a source of respect and trust, a requirement for leadership, and a foundation for many trade and business relationships. A Mende woman summarized the importance of membership: "If you don't belong to the secret soc [sic] up in the provinces, you cannot make any decisions, and you would be excluded from positions of authority, no matter how old you are….If you are not a member of the Society, oh I tell you, you feel so left out."[14]

The historical roots of the societies extend to well before colonial times. As a result, the Creoles—the landed population of freed slaves—have not traditionally participated in secret societies. Some Creoles regarded these groups as "backward"; in particular, Creoles have been critical of the tradition of circumcising both male and female inductees. In addition, there has been increased international pressure on female secret societies to discontinue circumcision in their initiation practices.[15]

The Colonization of Sierra Leone

The following section includes an overview of how Sierra Leone came to be colonized, by whom, and some legacies with a specific focus on prostitution, family law, and marriage. This context informs subsequent discussions of current sexual regulation and sexual ordering in Sierra Leone and the claim laid out in the introduction that current gender norms are partially reflective of Sierra Leone's colonial legacies. Sierra Leone's colonial era began with the establishment of Freetown as a British post and a settlement for former slaves in 1787. It was designated as an official crown colony in 1808.[16] Descriptions of the early years of colonial Sierra Leone vary from a stunning paradise to the "white man's grave"—in reference to the number of settlers who died of various tropical diseases.[17] With the help of the discovery and exploitation of natural resources, for years Sierra Leone flourished as a colony. As a result of landmarks such as the establishment of Fouray Bay College—the first university in western Africa—during the 1800s Freetown was deemed "the Athens of West Africa."

Sierra Leone's history has been shaped by waves of regional and international migration. In the early years of colonization, in addition to the colonizers and the indigenous tribal groups, Freetown became home to freed slaves from the Americas, slaves captured on shipping vessels by the British, Arab traders, a small number of British merchants, a powerful group of Lebanese traders, and British military personnel.[18] After the abolition of slavery, Freetown was designated as the future home for freed slaves. The diverse groups of Africans that arrived in Freetown as a result of the abolishment of slavery became uniformly known as Creoles. The Creole language was a confection inspired by English and the various dialects of the settlers.

British colonizers tended to distinguish the Creoles from "the natives"—or the some fourteen existing ethnic groups in Sierra Leone. The Creoles, or "trousered blacks,"[19] were considered an elite class largely because they had descended from liberated Africans who were seen to have "cultivated [Western/British] habits and [had] come to accept their way of living."[20] By some accounts, the British saw Creoles as partners in their mission to civilize West Africa.[21] This categorization, combined with the fact that most Creoles lived in the crown colony (the Freetown area) as opposed to "the provinces" (areas outside Freetown were not included in the colony until 1896), offered Creoles significant advantages over the rest of the population in Sierra Leone. According to the 1931 census, more than half of all children enrolled in schools lived in the Freetown area.[22] Although Creoles constitute only 2 to 3 percent of the current population in Sierra Leone today, they remain a significant portion of the country's political and economic elite.

Similar to other British colonial projects, one of the objectives for colonial administrators in Sierra Leone was to "civilize" the local population through education and the alteration or elimination of "traditional" social practices. Lansana Gberie has argued that the British regarded their colony in Sierra Leone as "an experiment in 'conversionism.'"[23] The tools of conversion included not only education but also the introduction of religion and legal codes to restrict colonial subjects. Historian Leo Spitzer summarized the colonizers' belief that "social redemption and elevation of submerged groups would not occur through the removal of legal disabilities alone: that the state or established religious, philanthropic or educated institutions would be required to bring about the integration and social adjustment of the emancipated."[24] The British enacted their moral superiority to justify their regulation of the colony, with the control of sexuality and the establishment of a particular form of conjugal order at the heart of governance strategies.

Colonization and Sexual Regulation

Authors such Richard Phillips have pointed to the connections between the regulation of sexuality and imperial power. In *Sex, Politics and Empire: A Postcolonial Geography*, Phillips concludes: "Colonisation schemes were organised around sexual arrangements."[25] Lenore Manderson also argues that colonial authorities used sex as a basis to justify what she calls the "moral logic of colonialism."[26] In particular, Mariarosa Dalla Costa has argued that colonizers worked to create and enforce the nuclear family unit because of the administration and economic benefits.[27] Harris also noted that the heterosexual nuclear family was considered the building block for the agricultural colonization of various parts of the world.[28]

Prostitution

An examination of the regulation of prostitution in colonial Sierra Leone can provide a useful glimpse into the priority that sexual regulation held for colonial administrators, the assumed moral superiority of the British, and the way in which the British characterized the African female subject. Josephine Butler, an advocate of legalizing prostitution in the British Empire, argued that "the way people and government treated prostitutes and other sexual outsiders—a category in which we might include sexually active younger people and those with lovers of the same sex or a different race—spoke volumes about their domestic and imperial society, about the way it was and the way they wanted it to be."[29] Prostitution was deemed a necessary aspect of colonial life in part due to the high number of single males sent to administer the colonies. Despite the acceptance of prostitution, there is a great deal of evidence indicating that colonial authorities were determined to regulate it.

Prostitution was generally regulated under contagious disease (CD) laws; however, these laws were never passed in Sierra Leone. This aberration in British colonial practice has been explained as a financial decision resulting from the prevalence and uncontrollability of prostitution in the country.[30] Instead of CD laws, the British enacted numerous regulations "to improve public morals" in Sierra Leone, including banning public nudity, dancing after dark, and walking or loitering in any thoroughfare or public place for the purposes of prostitution.[31] Prostitutes were not charged for their sexual activity; rather, they were charged with "loitering with intent."[32] The charge had nothing to do with a sexual act but was for walking publicly, indicating that the regulations surrounding prostitution had more to do with the regulation of women within public spaces than it did with sexual activity.

There are other indications that colonial governors wanted to control the public activity of African women in response to the perceived threatening potential of their unregulated sexual behavior. The image of the African subject as highly sexualized and lacking moral restraint informed both the specific regulations associated with prostitution and the general "moral logic" of colonial missions.[33] In fact, it can be argued that the legitimization of the colonial mission was dependent on the sexualization of the would-be colonial subject. Richard Burton's work exemplifies this argument. An English traveler and author, Burton concluded that there was a "great gulf, moral and physical, separating the black from the white races of man."[34] Burton's construction of African women as "vicious" and the men as "bestial" was said to have informed Sierra Leone's colonial officials. Burton's writings also influenced larger discourses on African sexuality and broader debates about the moral justification for colonialism at the time. In particular, Burton described Sierra Leone as a region of "primal disorder" characterized by "savagery" and immorality—a place "effectively awaiting colonization."[35]

Marriage

For the colonizers in Sierra Leone, the promotion of the heterosexual nuclear family model was a key colonial objective. Similar to learning to eat with knives and forks, and covering their bodies with clothing, colonial administrators and missionaries saw marriage as essential to the civilizing mission. There was a particular emphasis on eradicating polygamy and female circumcision and replacing "fluid" customary unions with legally defined marriages.[36] Colonial authorities devoted attention to enforcing recognized models of marriage, while missionaries and "purity campaigners" concentrated on marriage unions. In turn, marriage became what Kristin Mann called a "virtual obsession" in West Africa during the late nineteenth century.[37] An Anglican bishop summarized the church's position on marriage:

> The Great desideratum in the social life of the colony is the sanctity of the marriage relationship, and the creation and maintenance of home and family life . . . . the comparative absence of the ideas of love and fellowship from the marriage tie, utterly wrong views about the relative duties of husband and wife, tend to encourage concubinage, and this degrades women from her true place, becomes the fruitful source of strife and disunion, and children dragged up under these circumstances are apt to see and hear much that is most unfortunate.[38]

This quotation reiterates the significance of recognized, Christian marriages to the colonial project. Efforts to encourage recognized marriage—that is, legal marriage—did not end with the colonial period. Since the 1950s, the Sierra Leone government has made great efforts to standardize the various types of marriages that exist within the country. In a research report on family law in Sierra Leone conducted in the 1970s, the authors continued to portray marriage as a solution to social chaos: "The absence of an effective method of recognizing the legal status of these marriages leads to many problems, including problems of maintenance, legitimacy, bigamy and inheritance."[39]

Family Law

An analysis of the laws regulating the family today in Sierra Leone is complicated by the fact that, as a result of the damage and chaos caused by the conflict, as well as the lack of resources and attention given to maintaining records, many of these laws are "scattered around" or have "gone out of print."[40] This means, literally, that some copies of various legal documents cannot be located because the remaining paper copies of the documents are lost or have been destroyed.

The second source of complication stems from the initial separation of the official colony of Sierra Leone with the rest of the country, or "the provinces." The result of this bifurcation was that the vast majority of Sierra Leoneans were never under direct colonial rule and not subject to colonial law. This meant that customary law was, and continues to be, the most recognized system for the majority of Sierra Leoneans. Although customary law marriages were equated in law with civil and Christian marriages after 1965, there remain some essential differences among these forms, particularly in terms of inheritance rights and paternity rights.[41] Further information about the major types of marriages and marriage customs can be found in chapter 6, and a more detailed description and analysis of paternity, custody, and adoption laws is provided in chapter 5.

The Conflict

Numerous authors and researchers commenting on the conflict in Sierra Leone have concluded that these eleven years were the century's most violent and vicious.[42] In fact, explanations of the sources of the civil war are often overshadowed by fantastical descriptions of Sierra Leone as a location of unearthly Armageddon. Sierra Leone has been depicted by authors such as Robert Kaplan as "barbaric," exhibiting "new age primitivism," and "premodern."[43] Former British prime minister Tony Blair's foreign policy adviser Robert Cooper conveyed a seemingly common image of West Africa when he declared that the region, as a "pre-modern world of failed states...of 'barbarians, chaos and disorder,'" posing a threat to Western civilization because "it can provide a base for non-state actors who may represent a danger to the post-modern world."[44]

More cerebral accounts of Sierra Leone's history and conflict tend to link the sources of the conflict to the legacies of colonialism, international and local exploitation of resources, systemic government corruption, extreme poverty and inequality, and the outside influence of Charles Taylor and his troops from Liberia. David Keen argued that it was the combination of the absence of employment opportunities, growing poverty in the face of corruption, and a decrepit state that inspired men and women to join armed groups.[45] For Keen, rebel groups and the Sierra Leone Army offered protection and resources that were unavailable to civilians, making warfare attractive and lucrative for many young Sierra Leoneans. Lansana Gberie, a journalist who covered the Sierra Leone conflict, has written extensively about how rebels were enticed by the prospect of controlling the nation's diamond wealth. This hypothesis that diamonds were a central motivation behind the conflict has been supported by a number of experts, including Ibrahim Kamara, Sierra Leone's permanent representative to the UN during the conflict. Kamara has been quoted as saying that the root of his country's war "is, and remains diamonds, diamonds and diamonds."[46]

Fighting Forces

The main groups of fighting forces that were involved in the Sierra Leone conflict included the Revolutionary United Front (RUF), the Civil Defence Forces (CDF)—or the Kamajors, the Armed Forces Revolutionary Council (AFRC), and the Sierra Leone Army (SLA). The CDF was a paramilitary group that supported the Sierra Leone Army against the RUF. The CDF fought alongside and often mixed with the Kamajors, originally a Mende male hunting group that developed into a fighting faction to defend civilians. The Kamajors were often described as a mystical battle group because some believed that magical water and rituals would make them invincible to bullets. The Kamajors' name comes from *kamajoi*, a Mende word meaning hunter; although it was originally a male-only group, there are some indications that women participated as Kamajor soldiers. By March 1994 it was estimated that more than 500 Kamajors were involved in combat activity.[47] It has been argued that abuses conducted by the Kamajors during the war were largely overlooked because of their image as defenders of civilians.[48] There were also some concerns that the Kamajors were not included in the disarmament process at the end of the conflict.

The RUF is the most notorious armed group and was the dominant rebel force for the entire eleven-year conflict. It is reported that some original RUF rebel commanders such as Foday Sankoh received military training in Libya, although this link has been contested by a number of researchers.[49] The RUF was largely a product of Charles Taylor and his desire to influence the politics and diamond industry of Sierra Leone. Original members of the RUF were unemployed or underemployed young men who were attracted by promises of diamond wealth and political power. Throughout the conflict, the membership of the RUF expanded and diversified to include a large number of children (many abducted), women and girls, and disgruntled members of the national army. The stated objective of the RUF was to liberate civilians from a corrupt government; however, its mission became muddied and overshadowed by greed, violence, and brutal displays of power.[50] Several accounts of the RUF conclude that the group manifested disaster and horror rather than revolution.[51]

The Sierra Leone Army seemed to morph into a variety of forms over the years of the conflict. As already mentioned, a number of SLA members who were dissatisfied with low wages and poor conditions joined the RUF at various stages of the war. There were also members of the SLA who maintained their status as members of government forces but collaborated with RUF members and participated in rebel activity such as diamond mining, looting, and sexual violence. These "sobels"—soldiers by day and rebels by night—served to diminish the authority of the government and undermine civilian trust in government forces.

The SLA was supported by several groups throughout the civil war. The Economic Community of West African States Monitoring Group (ECOMOG) was sent in as an intervening force during the early stages of the conflict. Led by Nigerians, ECOMOG had several successes in Sierra Leone, including ousting the AFRC—a group of rebels that ousted an elected government and briefly held control of the country—in 1998 and maintaining control over the airport during the worst periods of the civil conflict. Despite the praises offered to ECOMOG, some blamed its inefficiency for the eventual brutal invasion of Freetown in January 1999; other reporters and civilians claimed that ECOMOG committed atrocities similar to those of the RUF during the conflict.

Executive Outcomes (EO) was another militant group from South Africa that was hired in 1995 by the leader of one of Sierra Leone's many coups, Captain Valentine Strasser of the National Provisional Ruling Council, to help control rebel activity. The EO included Angolans, Zimbabweans, and Namibians and was described by *Harper's* as "a collection of former spies, assassins, and crack bush guerrillas."[52] Finally, United Nations soldiers acting as part of the United Nations Mission in Sierra Leone (UNAMSIL) supported the Sierra Leone government and managed the disarmament process along with a cohort of British troops. About 110 International Mission and Training (IMAT) British troops continue to train SLA members today.

Conflict Time Lines

Although the manifold factions, coups, peace accords, and international interventions make it difficult to succinctly summarize the conflict, it is helpful to describe the war as occurring in several distinct periods: 1991 to 1996, 1996 to 1997, 1997 to 1998, January 1999, and February 1999 to January 2002. The first period, from 1991 to 1996, saw the beginnings of the conflict and two military coups, and ended with democratic elections. During most of this period, the deaths and destruction caused by fighting in Sierra Leone were largely ignored by the international community. The beginning of Sierra Leone's civil conflict is often cited as Charles Taylor's announcement on the BBC on November 1, 1990, threatening to attack and destroy Sierra Leone's airport. Taylor was distraught that Sierra Leone had allowed ECOMOG, whose mission was to control Taylor and his forces in Liberia, to be based in Sierra Leone.[53] After this announcement, the first RUF rebel forces—largely members of Taylor's own fighting factions—infiltrated Sierra Leone's eastern border areas.

Shortly after the RUF invasion, led by Corporal Foday Sankoh, the RUF launched an offensive on farmers, villagers, and miners. The objectives at this point were primarily to demonstrate the weakness of then president Joseph Momoh. Momoh struggled to recruit troops to help resist the RUF, resulting in a large number of young and untrained men joining the SLA. In April 1992 several junior officers of the SLA carried out a coup forcing Momoh to flee to Guinea. The National Provisional Ruling Council (NPRC) was formed as the ruling power with Captain Valentine Strasser as chairman. Although the NPRC was initially successful in pushing the RUF out of the diamond-rich areas and into Liberia, the RUF soldiers regrouped and returned with intensified attacks on civilians. The NPRC initiated another recruitment campaign that primarily attracted uneducated and untrained youths. Due to poor training and sporadic pay, this particular group of soldiers—or sobels—was frequently accused of looting, theft, and collaboration with the RUF.

From 1991 to 1996 the RUF gained power over the diamond areas in the east, terrorized and murdered countless civilians, looted and destroyed houses, schools, and hospitals, and systemically used sexual violence to terrorize populations. By 1996 more than 15,000 people had been killed, 70 percent of the country's schools had been destroyed, only eighty health centers were still functioning (mostly in Freetown), 900,000 citizens had registered for food aid, and nearly half of the population were displaced.[54] It was reported that by March 1996, 75 percent of school-age children were out of school, and the country's economy had shrunk to an annual growth rate of negative 6.24 percent.[55] At this time, Strasser relied heavily on Nigerian troops to protect Freetown and eventually hired Executive Outcomes to support the SLA.[56]

The years 1996–1997 constitute the second distinct period, beginning with a tenuous phase of stability and democratic elections. Through the help of EO and Nigerian troops, the RUF forces were contained and driven from Freetown in 1996.[57] At this time, despite RUF terror tactics, there was significant pressure from civil society groups, particularly women's groups, for elections to be held to replace the military government. Leading up to the elections the RUF used amputations to discourage citizens from voting. The mantra of the RUF at this time was "No hands to fingerprint, no fingerprints no vote." At the end of February 1996, presidential elections were held, and after a March run-off ballot Ahmad Tejan Kabbah won the presidency. Shortly after taking office, Kabbah initiated peace talks with the RUF in the Ivory Coast; however, the hope offered by these talks and by the Kabbah presidency was short-lived. In May 1997, just fifteen months after the elections, young and dissatisfied members of the SLA formed a group called the Armed Forces Revolutionary Council and launched another coup. Major Johny Paul Koroma, who was being held in prison awaiting trial for treason, was declared the leader of this group after troops streamed into Freetown and opened the Pademba Road prison, releasing Koroma along with more than 600 prisoners.[58] The AFRC declared that it wanted to form an alliance with RUF members and encouraged rebels to join its movement.

The next period of the conflict, from May 1997 to March 1998, was described as "bloody chaos"[59] and a "normative collapse of the long suffering Sierra Leone state."[60] Journalists opposing the AFRC ruling regime were threatened and tortured, the disarmament process that had been initiated was rejected by the new government, and widespread violence and terror escalated. Understandably, there was a massive national rejection of the AFRC, with approximately 400,000 Sierra Leoneans deciding to flee during the first three months of the coup. Although the AFRC promised to retain power until 2001, ECOMOG troops increased their number of forces and pressured the AFRC to negotiate a peace deal. After a military embargo and growing pressure, the AFRC agreed to reinstate Kabbah by April 1998. By February 1998, ECOMOG troops had taken control of Freetown and attempted to secure the capital for Kabbah's return in March. Upon Kabbah's return, he announced his third cabinet at the end of March while continuing to rely heavily on ECOMOG troops to maintain security.

Despite diplomatic efforts by the reinstated president, the security situation in Sierra Leone continued to deteriorate until, out of fear and desperation, international agencies and the UN began withdrawing foreign staff in December 1998. On January 6, three days after the United Nations Observation Mission in Sierra Leone (UNOMSIL) mission evacuated its last members from the country, rebel groups initiated what was easily the most brutal attack of the entire conflict. On this day RUF forces descended on Freetown in what was called "Operation No Living Thing."[61] The motivation for the attack was unclear but may have included the objective of releasing Foday Sankoh from Pademba Road prison. In a sick twist of fate, rebel forces raided a World Food Program warehouse outside of Freetown before the attack and found hundreds of new machetes that had been purchased for farming tools. Instead of being used for cultivation, these machetes became the primary weapons for hundreds of rebel forces, resulting in multiple amputations and slayings. During this attack on the capital, it is estimated that more than 5,000 civilians were killed, 3,000 children were reported missing, and one-third of the total population was homeless.[62] Although the full scope of the horror of these days cannot be summarized here, Gberie's account provides an effective glimpse into the events:

> Civilians were gunned down within their houses, rounded up and massacred on the streets, thrown from the upper floors of buildings, used as human shields, and burnt alive in cars and houses. They had their limbs hacked off with machetes, eyes gouged out with knives, hands smashed with hammers, and bodies burned with boiling water. Women and girls were systematically sexually abused, and children and young people abducted by the hundreds.[63]

If anything beneficial could be seen as resulting from this campaign of terror, it was that the international community finally turned its attention to Sierra Leone. The UN approved a peacekeeping contingent of 6,000 that was authorized to use deadly force.

On July 7, 1999, the Lomé Peace Accord was signed between the Sierra Leone government and the major fighting forces. The accord had serious problems: rebel forces were pardoned for the atrocities they had committed, and, shockingly, the RUF's Foday Sankoh was appointed director of the National Resources Commission—giving him control over the country's diamond industry.[64] The phase that followed this accord up until the end of the conflict in January 2002 was perhaps the most trying time in the history of UN peacekeeping. UNAMSIL's commitment following "Operation No Living Thing" was welcomed by the citizens of Sierra Leone, but the peacekeepers were ill matched and ill prepared for rebel activity. UNAMSIL soldiers were only lightly armed and, initially, could not use force unless under direct threat. As a result, there were several reports of civilians being killed by rebel forces while UN soldiers could merely watch. The peacekeepers failed to convince both civilians and rebels of their authority in the country. UNAMSIL was referred to as "U-nasty" and peacekeepers were called "beachkeepers" because cohorts could often be found enjoying the country's beaches.[65] The disarmament process had slowed to a near halt due to a lack of coordination by peacekeepers and bullying by RUF soldiers. UNAMSIL troops also failed to prevent the virtual failure of the Lomé Peace Accord.

The UN has been accused of rendering West Africa a "laboratory for the United Nations (UN) peacekeeping."[66] The UN mission in Sierra Leone had been watched by the international community with great interest and scrutiny not only because it was the largest UN peacekeeping mission in history—before the mission ended its troop numbers exceeded 20,000—but also because it was contrasted to concurrent missions of the United States in Somalia and the UN mission in Kosovo. There is no denying that the UN mission in Sierra Leone went through a steep learning curve during its first few years. Perhaps the greatest challenge came in 2000 when RUF soldiers kidnapped 500 UNAMSIL peacekeepers.[67] The kidnapping was a response to the refusal of the UN to accede to the RUF's demand for the return of ten fighters who had given up their weapons during the disarmament process. The kidnapping of UN troops was humiliating for the relatively new and ambitious mission in Sierra Leone. The international community began to question the role of the UN and its relevance and capabilities in conflict zones. This pressure led to a rethinking of UNAMSIL and the institution of reforms to the mission—the most significant was the mandate to kill RUF soldiers as the situation required and to accelerate the disarmament process. Despite its challenges, over time the mission has become largely viewed as a success and a model for future interventions.[68]

The Official "End" of Conflict

There was no single event or peace accord that ended conflict in Sierra Leone. There are claims (particularly by British soldiers) that British troops sent in after the embarrassment of the UN kidnapping ordeal effectively "cleaned up" UNAMSIL's mess and restored peace. There are other claims that general war fatigue, combined with the increasing effectiveness of UNAMSIL and British soldiers, led to the surrender of RUF fighters: "The RUF probably thought that the UN peace process was more attractive than dealing with British troops and the Sierra Leone government forces."[69] With the ending of the adult disarmament process in January 2002,[70] President Kabbah declared the war over.[71] By this time 72,490 adult combatants had been disarmed and 42,000 weapons were collected.[72] In July 1999, through the Lomé Peace Accord, the Truth and Reconciliation Commission (TRC) had been initiated to produce "an impartial body of historical record" of the war and to "help restore the human dignity of the victims and promote reconciliation."[73] Although it was criticized for its timing, its Eurocentric focus, the lack of dissemination, and its narrowness, the 50,000-page TRC report was released in October 2004.

The Disarmament, Demobilization, and Reintegration Process

The following are the most common definitions of each of the three phases of the disarmament, demobilization, and reintegration process: first, disarmament is "the collection of small arms and light and heavy weapons within a conflict zone"; second, demobilization is the "process by which parties to a conflict begin to disband their military structures, and combatants begin the transformation into civilian life"[74]; finally, reintegration is "the process which allows ex-combatants and their families to adapt economically and socially to productive civilian life." In 1998, in the midst of continued violence and insecurity, the government of Sierra Leone announced it had designed a plan for national disarmament. The Sierra Leone government and the World Bank established the Multi-Donor Trust Fund (MDTF) to solicit funding from the international donor community for the DDR, with the World Bank, UNICEF, UNAMSIL, and the Sierra Leone government providing a significant portion of the funding. The National Committee for Disarmament, Demobilization and Reintegration (NCDDR) was created to oversee the three-phase process of disarmament, demobilization, and reintegration. The ultimate goal declared by the NCDDR was "to support the national strategy for peace that include[d] the consolidation of the political process and security, which form the basis for a viable post-war national recovery programme."[75] The initial mandate was to target 45,000 soldiers from the Revolutionary United Front, the Civil Defence Forces, and the Sierra Leone Army; however, by the time the program finished its mandate in 2002, more than 75,000 combatants were disarmed at more than sixteen demobilization centers around the country.[76]

Those who went through the DDR were given vocational skills training in one of the following areas: carpentry, metalworking, auto mechanics, tailoring, fabric dyeing, soap making, hairdressing, plumbing and masonry, electrical works, computer skills, building material production, and basic construction and technology. Training in all areas typically lasted between three and nine months, depending on the trade.[77] The apprentice program offered similar trades and was designed for those with limited education. Other initiatives included special programs for child ex-combatants and disabled ex-combatants and "family stabilization measures," including microcredit programs for the wives of ex-combatants and female ex-combatants.[78]

According to NCDDR statistics, 39 percent of ex-combatants chose formal education, 23 percent chose skills training, 10 percent chose an apprenticeship, and approximately 4 percent chose public works and job placement.[79] In addition, about 2,385 ex-RUF and CDF soldiers were recruited into the Sierra Leone Army.[80] Although the NCDDR did not investigate the numbers of males and females enrolled in the assorted trades, interviews with staff and facilitators of training programs in Sierra Leone indicate that women and girls enrolled almost exclusively in either fabric dyeing, soap making, tailoring, catering, hairdressing, or weaving.[81] In addition, the few programs that targeted female soldiers as beneficiaries consistently offered these select trades.[82]

Looking Back

At the end of the DDR, the government of Sierra Leone declared that "all the armed units of both the RUF and the CDF were disarmed."[83] The improvement of security in the country was deemed the greatest achievement of the disarmament process. The international community largely saw the process as a success and even recommended using the Sierra Leone DDR as a model for future post-conflict situations. Despite earning praises, each phase of the DDR had significant flaws. Funding was perhaps the most consistent obstacle to the successful implementation of the DDR. There are a variety of reasons as to why the DDR in Sierra Leone was constantly destitute, including the gross underestimation of the number of ex-combatants who would arrive for disarmament. Also, perhaps because Kosovo and East Timor were receiving more attention and more funding, only half of the needed $50 million had been donated to the Sierra Leone DDR by the end of 1999.[84] Funding shortfalls led to difficulties such as insufficient camp provisions at demobilization centers, delayed payments to ex-combatants, and the slow establishment of demobilization centers.

Particular concerns with the disarmament stage of the DDR included inadequate information about the armed groups in Sierra Leone and the challenge of ongoing violence and insecurity. Francis Kai-Kai, executive secretary of the NCDDR, admitted that "right from the planning phase, it was difficult to get reliable military information on troop strength, location and quantity of weapons in possession of respective fighting forces."[85] Without this information, the NCDDR had difficulty estimating the total number of forces in particular areas, the number of children, and the number of female soldiers. This imprecision complicated the planning and implementation of the entire DDR. Security was a major concern during the disarmament period. Throughout the first phase of the DDR more than 50 percent of the country was inaccessible due to violence and the RUF control of territory.[86] During some periods, the RUF even managed to prohibit UNAMSIL from operating in eastern areas. There were also reports that Foday Sankoh and other RUF commanders were preventing their troops from participating in the disarmament.

The demobilization phase of the DDR also faced distinct obstacles. The organization of the demobilization phase led to misunderstandings and tension between combatants and facilitators. A significant number of combatants who had been disarmed never completed the demobilization process. Some combatants were intimidated by the photo identification process that was established and believed the data would be used to prosecute them later. As will be discussed further in chapter 4, women were particularly apt to leave demobilization centers due to a lack of security or stigma. Not all demobilization centers had separate areas for women and girls, and sexual violence was reported as a concern at numerous locations.

Criticisms of the reintegration phase of the DDR primarily emphasize funding shortcomings and the limitations of training programs. The goal of providing all combatants with skills to support themselves financially was obstructed by inadequate funding for programs and the extreme destruction of the national economy. Abbreviated reintegration programs graduated combatants who were not only poorly trained but also trained in skills that were often useless in their home region or community. The NCDDR admitted the need for an assessment of "the relevance of the various skills area in the context of the needs of the economy."[87] However, a labor market analysis was never consulted during the implementation of the reintegration programs. As discussed in chapter 4, women were greatly impacted by the limited training options offered to them. Although reports indicate that combatants were free to choose any of the trades offered, there are strong indications that women and girls were expected to choose one of the highly gendered options mentioned earlier. Sulay Sesay, one of the coordinators for the DDR, recounted that he could recall only one woman enrolled in the male-dominated trades.[88]

War and Sexual Violence

Throughout the conflict, rape, sexual violence, and sexual slavery were primary tactics of warfare. The Truth and Reconciliation Commission report recorded the testimonies of more than 800 women and girls who had been raped. These women and girls represent a small portion of the total estimated number of victims of sexual violence. According to Physicians for Human Rights, more than 200,000 women and girls may have been victims of rape during the conflict in Sierra Leone. When Physicians for Human Rights conducted a specific study among 991 internally displaced women and their family members, it found that 94 percent of respondents had experienced some exposure to war-related violence and 13 percent had experienced war-related sexual assault.[89] Although rape was used throughout the eleven-year conflict, a higher number of incidents were reported during the 1999 rebel incursion into Freetown. Between March 1999 and March 2000, a total of 2,350 rape survivors were registered in Freetown alone during the Forum for African Women Educationalists (FAWE) Rape Victims Programme.[90] Of these survivors, 2,085 were between the ages of zero and twenty-six, and 165 were older than twenty-seven.[91] It was reported that "many" other victims of sexual violence did not come forward for treatment.[92]

Women and War

One of the downsides to the publicity surrounding sexual violence and the Sierra Leone conflict is that it helped to create a general picture of women and girls exclusively as victims of the conflict. Many accounts of the war describe women as victims of sexual violence or sex slaves, victims of the economic impacts of war, or captives of their rebel commanders. The Lomé Peace Accord mentions only female victims and does not even make reference to female soldiers. Although women and girls were certainly victimized in unimaginable ways, their experience of, and participation in, the war was not merely as victims. Little is written about women and girls as agents within the civil conflict; however, there is evidence that women—particularly female soldiers—were empowered through their roles in the conflict.

Some of the various activities that women and girls were reported to have participated in during the war include killing, using weapons, commanding armed groups, spying, looting, raping, and burning houses.[93] In some cases women were reported to have dressed in rich clothing and lived for months in villages the RUF was planning to attack.[94] There are other stories of powerful female commanders such as Adama Cut-Hand, who was said to be among the most brutal RUF members. Other famous female warriors include Marie Keita and Willimina Bintu Fofana, who were said to have mystical powers against bullets.[95] Edward Anague, director of a small organization called the Community Extension Development Association (CEDA), reported that "some of the most vicious soldiers and commanders were women."[96] Despite this evidence, there are still huge gaps in terms of what we know about female soldiers in Sierra Leone. Specifically, there are conflicting statistics on the number of female soldiers and varying reports of the roles that women played as soldiers.

It is nearly impossible to be absolutely certain of the exact number of female soldiers who participated in the Sierra Leone conflict. Most estimates are based on disarmament data, or numbers provided by NGOs or individual researchers. By comparing exit data from the disarmament program with other reports on the numbers of female soldiers during the conflict, we now know that the majority of female soldiers did not participate in the program. The numbers are further complicated by estimates of the number of women in particular armed groups such as the RUF, the Civil Defence Forces, the AFRC, child soldier ranks, and the Sierra Leone Army. Estimates of females within particular fighting factions are not always helpful because they have been confused with the total number of female soldiers.

Most of the estimates of women's involvement in the war are derived from the number of women in the RUF. Of the total number of RUF soldiers demobilized (24,352), Conciliation Resources, an independent charity working internationally to end violence and promote peace, has estimated that the number of women soldiers may have been 10,000.[97] This same source estimates that up to 9,500 of these women may have been abducted or donated by relatives. Myriam Denov has reported that up to 30 percent of RUF child soldiers were girls.[98] As indicated in chapter 3, my own data indicate that anywhere from 30 to 50 percent of the various factions of fighting forces during the conflict in Sierra Leone were females.

Also discussed in chapter 3 is the effort made post-conflict to differentiate female soldiers from female abductees, camp followers, sex slaves, and domestic workers. It was often assumed that women and girls fell within one of the later categories and were seldom categorized solely as soldiers. Despite this, there is growing evidence that women and girls took part in all aspects of conflict—including combat. Due to the lack of information and reliable statistics about the number of female soldiers, reintegration programs—including training programs, counseling, health care, and family tracing—for these women and girls were insufficient or nonexistent. Andy Brooks argues that post-conflict reintegration programs tend to be based on the assumption that male adolescents are the primary beneficiaries.[99] The few programs directed at females after the conflict tended to target female victims, abductees, or sexual violence victims rather than female soldiers. UNICEF's Girls Left Behind program defined its beneficiaries as women and girl *abductees* who were associated with the fighting forces but did not benefit from the disarmament process. Further, in the UN report *From Peacekeeping to Peacebuilding: UN Strategy to Support National Recovery and Peacebuilding in Sierra Leone*, in a section on child protection issues, it is recommended that the UN "assist and support girls/young women who were *forcibly abducted* and are being prevented from returning home."[100]

The impact of major programs such as this was that only women and girls who fit the list of "acceptable" roles during the conflict were eligible for benefits post-conflict. There were no specific programs for violent women or women leaders, for example. The lack of programs targeting women and girls soldiers who voluntarily joined served to define "female soldier" as someone who was a victim, captured by men, and forced to serve with an armed group. A further impact is that statistics gathered from such programs may be skewed as a result of women and girls adjusting their wartime stories and experiences in order to qualify for the desperately needed benefits of reintegration programs.

Moving Forward

One of the objectives of this chapter was to provide an overview of colonial and postcolonial sexual regulation and its legacies. An understanding of the way in which sex, marriage, and childbirth have been regulated throughout Sierra Leone's colonial and postcolonial period helps contextualize current conjugal order, social relations, stereotypes, and hierarchies. The following chapters will move from this general introduction to Sierra Leone to a more specific analysis of particular issues related to "post-conflict" development. A second objective of the chapter was to signal the magnitude and complexity of the civil conflict in Sierra Leone. Appreciating the various phases, actors, tactics, motivations, and strategies of the conflict disrupts portrayals of the conflict as merely irrational unabated chaos. Likewise, details of the conflict support the claim that one-size-fits-all post-conflict policies, such as the DDR model, are blunt instruments that do not necessarily address the specific causes, events, or impacts of particular conflicts.

3

Defining Soldiers

Tryphena, a girl soldier who was with the RUF for two years and seven months, is nicknamed Wanda-dai. In Krio, Wanda-dai means one who has tasted or nearly missed death. It also is a common way of expressing negative experiences that one managed to survive and implies that a person "went to hell but came back, or died once but is alive again."[1] Tryphena arrived at the Children Associated with the War (CAW) facilities with a bullet wound in the left side of her neck. It appeared to have just missed her spinal cord. She was complaining to CAW officials of pain in her throat. She gave the following account of her time with the rebels: "I was abducted during the rebel attack in 1997 and was forced to join the RUF. I was trained to fire a weapon. I was locked up in a house that was set ablaze. I tried to escape but was shot [in] the neck/throat. I was abandoned in a separate house because of the smell of my sore." In addition to her training with, and use of, weapons, she reported destroying property and using drugs while with the RUF. Tryphena told CAW staff that she was in school before the war and that she believes her parents are alive.

Female soldiers wholly disrupt gendered binaries associated with war, particularly the contrasting image of the male warrior and female victim. Furthermore, female soldiers challenge dominant war mythologies, including the myth that women are naturally peaceful and men are naturally violent or heroic. Acknowledging that female soldiers exist requires a radical rethinking of prevailing war narratives as well as a substantial reorganization of post–armed conflict and peace-building policies. Despite ample evidence that females participated in the conflict, policy makers in Sierra Leone largely refused to acknowledge these women and girls and name them as beneficiaries, or as subjects worthy of policy attention. The resistance to recognizing female participation in war has mainly resulted from gendered norms and assumptions associated with conjugal order, including the idea that women are naturally peaceful due to their life-giving roles and the notion that men, as heads of households, are the decision makers and the sole political actors within armed movements.

Throughout the chapter I outline the resistance to acknowledging women's and girls' participation as soldiers during the civil war in Sierra Leone and the ways in which female soldiers are categorized as atypical. This chapter demonstrates that even when women participate in the activities of "high politics," or sectors traditionally categorized as security priorities such as war, they are effectively shuffled out of the public political sphere and into the domestic realm through post-conflict development policies. Female soldiers in Sierra Leone were (re)constructed as "wives," "camp followers," or "sex slaves" in order to desecuritize them, silence them, distinguish them from securitized male soldiers, and justify policies that either disregarded them or encouraged them to return to a highly gendered order.

Post-conflict programs in Sierra Leone, like similar failed programs in countries such as Angola and the Democratic Republic of the Congo, were inadequate primarily because they were based on the assumption that women are naturally peaceful while men should be the target of post-conflict development initiatives and security reform. These policies were not only inadequate; they served as a form of violence against women and girls post–armed conflict. In this chapter I argue that recasting women and girls from political activists and major contributors to the war to helpless victims and wounded, reluctant assistants is a form of violent reproduction. In the case of Sierra Leone, the construction of females post-conflict as victims lacking agency has dismissed, isolated, and silenced a vast cohort of women and girls who participated as soldiers. In addition, this construction relegates them spatially to the private realm—well away from the attention given to securitized and politicized matters by post-conflict policy makers.

This chapter builds on the argument made in the introduction that development policies serve to construct particular gendered identities. Lene Hansen's view of identity formation is employed to critique the construction of women and girl soldiers in Sierra Leone as helpless and passive victims "associated with the war" rather than political actors central to civil war activities. Hansen argues that identities are constructed through a process of linking and differentiation. I explore how particular notions of conjugal order inform the process of linking and differentiation between *securitized* male soldiers and *naturalized* female victims in Sierra Leone.

The construction of "soldier" by post-conflict policy makers in Sierra Leone can be understood as a process of exclusion whereby the term is defined in relation to a securitized male in contrast to a presumed desecuritized and naturally peaceful female. I argue that this construction of male soldiers assumes that men are naturally dominant and violent and defines them as securitized subjects and, therefore, as a priority for disarmament and post-conflict reconstruction programs. This is contrasted to the manner in which women and girls—even those who participated as soldiers—are characterized as either victims or naturally peaceful. These assumptions relegate females not only out of so-called security priorities and security sector reform but off the radar of "normal" post-conflict politics.

This chapter begins with an overview of how women and girls have typically been constructed both within mainstream literature on war and within criminology literature. I compare how the construction of perpetrators within the criminology literature and soldiers within literature on war requires the construction of an oppositional victim. In both cases, women and girls are often constructed as the "ideal victim." I explore the tendencies within both these literatures to essentialize both victim and perpetrator by implying that perpetrators are always perpetrators and never victims, and victims are always victims and never perpetrators. I argue that this binary is not helpful in understanding the experiences of either male or female soldiers because there is evidence that most soldiers both perpetrated atrocities and were victimized through experiences such as physical violence or abuse, sexual violence, and/or the death of a loved one.

The analysis of "ideal" victimhood is followed by a discussion of what is known about women's and girls' participation in Sierra Leone's war and how these female soldiers defined themselves. Here, first-person interviews with female soldiers, interview data with local NGO staff, disarmament experts, and social workers, and child intake forms from a local organization are utilized to create a picture of women's and girls' participation in the war. Next, this chapter features the efforts that have been made by both local and international organizations and agencies to label female soldiers as anything but soldiers. First-person interviews with Sierra Leonean social workers and experts on post–armed conflict reconstruction and disarmament, along with data from intake forms of unaccompanied children, are utilized to demonstrate how women and girls who clearly participated in military activities were classified into categories such as "women associated with the fighting forces," "abductees," "unaccompanied children," "bush wives," and "camp followers." These "nonsoldier" titles all assume a lack of agency and victimhood and deny the active role of females in combat.

In the final section, I consider the multiple impacts of excluding women and girls from the category of soldier in Sierra Leone. I argue that securitized subjects, such as soldiers, receive significantly more attention and funding from post-conflict policy makers. Furthermore, female soldiers serve to dislocate dominant war myths and gendered assumptions about what individuals do, and should do, during war. Ignoring female soldiers or reclassifying them into "non-soldier" categories reinforces dominant war myths and stereotypes, reproduces an inaccurate account of the war, leads to policies that discriminate against female soldiers, and sends moralizing messages about female soldiers as exceptions rather than legitimate subjects.

Moving beyond the Victim/Perpetrator Dichotomy

The literature on security and warfare gives the reader the distinct impression that "men make war, women make peace."[2] Aid agencies and military and peacekeeping operations have historically based their operations on the assumption that women and children are the most vulnerable victims of conflict.[3] Women's peaceful nature and their perceived aversion to risk[4] are sometimes described as stemming from their natural capacity as mothers[5]. In effect, roles that are depicted as natural for women during conflict are often associated with their reproductive capacities and their ability to nurture, cooperate, and sustain life. Instead of soldiering, women's primary roles during conflicts tend to be described as "wives, girlfriends, and mothers, waiting for their soldiers to return and caring for wounded."[6]

Across the continent of Africa, specifically, there is evidence that women have participated in civil wars, liberation struggles, organized resistance movements, protests, and political violence for decades.[7] Despite the burgeoning research on women's participation in armed movements, the message that "men are natural soldiers and women are not" remains prominent in many mainstream accounts of war, including the media, and government and NGO reports.

Although it is indisputable that women and girls as well as men and boys experienced trauma, abuse, malnourishment, fear, and neglect, the manner in which females are consistently and continually portrayed as victims— often helpless victims—must be critically examined. Criminology literature is useful in examining how both "victim" and "perpetrator" have traditionally been characterized in relation to women. Historically in criminology literature, the "ideal victim" has been defined as a powerless woman or girl.[8] Esther Madriz describes the stereotypical victim as a respectable woman who is weaker than her attacker and attacked while engaged in a "respectable" activity and at an "appropriate" time.[9] Madriz also points out that while female victims comply with the notion of "ideal" victim, women perpetrators deviate from norms associated with so-called feminine behavior. In fact, Merry Morash has concluded that "females who do not conform to common ideas about appropriate and moral behavior and appearance for girls and women are sometimes not taken seriously as victims or are blamed for their own victimization."[10]

Emblematic understandings of victim and perpetrator are not neutral but are shaped by gendered assumptions about suitable behaviors and so-called normal social order. Victim and perpetrator have become understood as mutually exclusive and oppositional gendered categories.[11] Thus, the distinction between perpetrator and victim encodes "appropriate" gender roles for males and females. By doing so, an entire set of norms and stereotypes that exert informal control over women and girls are sustained.[12] Within the literature on war, understandings of victims and perpetrators either obscure female perpetrators or classify them as exceptions. Furthermore, this binary between victim and perpetrator makes it equally difficult to conceive of male victims, or individuals who were both perpetrators and victims.

For the case of Sierra Leone, much of the literature and media analysis reproduces the victim/perpetrator binary by either ignoring women and girls or exclusively depicting them as victims. In some cases, the attention given to the widespread use of sexual violence by all warring parties during the civil war in Sierra Leone has eclipsed investigations into female soldiers and female perpetrators. Reports by organizations such as Amnesty International[13] and Physicians for Human Rights[14] are extremely valuable in providing rare insights into the extent of sexual violence in Sierra Leone; however, unbalanced attention to this aspect of the war has contributed to a narrow perception of women and girls solely as victims of the conflict.

The international humanitarian response to Sierra Leone's conflict has also concentrated on female victims. There are numerous examples of internationally supported programs directed at female victims of conflict; however, few programs (in fact almost none) targeted former female combatants. Unfortunately, there are also numerous media accounts of the conflict that depict women and girls solely as victims. In a gender profile conducted by AFROL news, the only independent news agency focusing exclusively on Africa, it was reported that "women and children are however known to be the principal war victims, often submitted to rape, sexual slavery, forced labour, torture, mutilation and forced recrutiation [sic] by the RUF

[Revolutionary United Front], known to use terror against the civil population as one of their principal war tactics."[15] Another report identified women as the "worst losers" of Sierra Leone's war. This article claimed: "Women [are] the symbol of love, kindness, mercy and spend their life coping with sexual and mental abuses done by one or more men in countries dealing with war like situation [sic]."[16]

Desecuritizing Women

Gendered assumptions about ideal victims and perpetrators have had obvious policy implications. In Sierra Leone, women and girls—regardless of whether they participated in the conflict—were rarely considered a security concern and were therefore not a central priority for post-conflict policy makers. In contrast, males are equally stereotyped as dangerous, and a potential risk to peace-building and security. Programs designed to address the destruction of social networks in Sierra Leone provide an interesting example of the variance in how males and females were conceptualized by post-conflict policy makers.

NGO and aid agency documents often refer to the destruction of social networks and norms as one of the most significant outcomes of the civil conflict in Sierra Leone. Duffield argues that NGOs "often frame their projects post-conflict in terms of re-establishment of social cohesion."[17] He contends that the representation of cultural breakdown gives impetus to NGOs and funding agencies to introduce and justify "new forms of identity and social cohesion."[18] Thus, programs aimed at reconstructing social networks benefit from depictions of local or indigenous relationships and customs as eroded or collapsed.

"Idle youth" are identified as a particular concern for the social reconstruction of Sierra Leone. Similar to many other countries, "idleness" in Sierra Leone was described as a problem almost exclusively in relation to men and boys. Specific concerns included the fear that these men and boys would reorganize or "let loose" and instigate another conflict or participate in organized crime.[19] The World Bank has defined the term "youth" in this context as referring to "predominantly men who are excluded, unable to provide for a family and are perceived as a potential *security threat*."[20] Several presumptions are at play in this definition: first, men are seen to be naturally violent; second, it is implied that if men are left to their own devices—without the nurturing, calming, or balancing influence of a wife or a mother—they may take up arms again or join in organized crime. Certain accounts conclude that cohorts of idle men caused the outbreak of war in Sierra Leone in the first place, and idleness could lead to another war.[21]

Although rare, policy makers have also analyzed the impacts of social disorder for women and girls in Sierra Leone. There are indications of displaced and unemployed, or "idle," women and girls; however, these females are not characterized as security threats. Instead, the concern for this cohort is that poverty, combined with the lack of social norms and regulations, will lead them to prostitution. One account of post-conflict Sierra Leone indicated, "Because of extreme poverty, the dislocation of families and the breakdown of social structures during the war, many girls, and some boys, are engaging in prostitution and sex in exchange for economic and other benefits."[22] Another report noted that it was "particularly those displaced from their homes and with few resources [who] resorted to prostitution as a means to support themselves and their children."[23]

While there is concern that idle men will become violent, the greatest concern regarding idle women and girls is their participation in prostitution. The logic seems to be that men are naturally aggressive and may manipulate this power in desperate situations whereas women are naturally nurturing and may manipulate their bodies in desperate situations. Put another way, under conditions of collapsed or absent social regulations, men will become violent while women will become overtly sexual. The result of this moralizing characterization is that male subjects in post-conflict programming are prioritized as a security priority while women are regarded as a social concern. These characterizations sustain gendered binaries associated with war. Furthermore, this understanding of idleness implies that men and women who disrupt conjugal order by delinking from the family unit and straying from "legitimate" and productive activities are delinquent and a source of social insecurity.

Female Soldiers Define Themselves

In this section I review the following four central conclusions that were drawn from interviews with former female soldiers in Sierra Leone: first, that the majority of "women and girls associated with the fighting forces" define themselves as soldiers; second, these female soldiers participated in multiple and diverse roles; third, female soldiers were often perpetrators of violence, destruction, and crime as well as victims of abuses such as sexual violence, abduction, and injury; finally, these interviews indicate that the number of females soldiers was much higher than existing estimations.[24]

Of the women interviewed in Sierra Leone, each responded positively to the question "Would you define yourself as a former soldier?" Women were quick to point out which armed group they were a part of, what rank they held, and what roles they carried out: one woman identified herself as a commander with the RUF; another woman specified that she was a soldier "because [she] was given one week training on how to fire a gun and subsequently became active";[25] a young woman identified herself as a soldier because she "took part in most of the horrible activities of the evil conflict in SL";[26] and several women admitted that they voluntarily joined a particular faction.

The duties carried out by this group of women were incredibly diverse. When asked, "What were your role(s) during the conflict?" more than 75 percent of the women I interviewed declared that they were involved in active combat duties. Respondents listed a variety of activities when asked what their roles were during the war, including "leading lethal attacks," "screening and killing pro-rebel civilians," "combatant," "poison/inject captured war prisoners with either lethal injection or acid," "I trained with [the AFRC] bush camp how to shoot a gun," "killing and maiming pro-government forces and civilians," "gun trafficking," "killing," "planning and carrying out attacks on public places," "do execution on commanders of my age group," "fighting," "murdered children," and "weapon cleaner."[27] One child soldier, Tina, "was abducted by the RUF when they attacked Kono, precisely Koidu town." She explained her activities during the two years she was with the RUF rebels: "I was trained to fire weapons, to be a security guard. I looted items and walked long distances on foot." She also reported that she destroyed property and partook in drug abuse as a soldier. The variety of responses to this question indicate the range of the roles carried out by women during the war. These responses also disrupt any strict gendered notions about the roles of women during conflict. From these interviews it becomes clear that women and girls participated in all facets of war, including active combat, commanding, and military training.

In addition to combat roles, many women and girls performed what has been classified by some as "support roles." These often include cooking, carrying war booty, food, or ammunition, spying, and taking care of the sick or children. The majority of women and girls also reported that they worked as sex slaves for either a particular commander or portions of their military unit. It should be noted that both males and females performed these support roles; however, the emphasis on distinguishing between combatants and supporters has focused primarily on female soldiers—few organizations or policy makers have spent time debating whether male soldiers were "real" soldiers or just acting in support roles. Policy makers and academics alike seem fixated on whether women and girls used weapons and were involved in active combat. Other forms of labor and activities contributing to the war effort are classified as "support roles" and distinguished from soldiering.

The logical maneuvering that categorizes females out of the rank of soldier goes something like this: most females acted in support roles for the fighting forces rather than in combat roles. Therefore females were primarily noncombatants—and, noncombatants are not soldiers. This logic is fallacious both because of the problematic assumption that women and girls were not combatants and because it implies that the support work carried out by females during conflict does not render them soldiers. Vivi Stavrou summarizes the implications of not recognizing various types of labor during the conflict:

> Not labeling the work of non-combatant women soldiers as soldiering, continues the gender discrimination of the division of labor whereby critical work that is essential for survival, is simply considered a natural extension of women's domestic obligations and hence neither worthy of remuneration nor significant enough for women to qualify for training and livelihoods programs.[28]

Even though the term "soldier" refers to anyone who is a member of an armed group, questions and concerns over the distinction between "combatant" and "soldier" have been raised in relation to women and girls. A review of the capacities, ranks, and services of any army reveals that a variety of duties and contributions are required for almost all combat operations; however, typically there are few who question whether male officers who fulfill support roles such as medical operations or communications are "real soldiers." When men act as porters, cleaners, domestic help, or messengers during war, there is little debate about the extent to which they deserve the soldier title. However, there has been extensive debate about the functions of female soldiers in Sierra Leone and the extent to which their work "counts" as soldiering. While great effort was made by post-conflict policy makers to name women and girls something other than soldiers, "men involved with the military in support functions are defined as soldiers, and not as 'men involved in armed groups or forces,' or as men directly associated with the war;' or as dependants of male or female combatants."[29]

In particular, the distinction between combatant and supporter is not useful for three reasons. First, it prioritizes the use of weapons among the other forms of labor that contribute to an armed movement. Warfare does not merely involve individuals with guns. Those who use guns and kill may be the most visible and may seem to make the most impact during a conflict; however, these combatants depend on an entire network of individuals and forms of labor to operate.

Second, these distinctions offer a narrow view of the kinds of actions performed by soldiers during war. The distinction between combatant and supporter seems to be based on traditional notions of warfare as a "man-to-man" public battle featuring "legitimate" or conventional weapons. This depiction simply does not capture most civil war activity. In Sierra Leone machetes and other homemade or rudimentary weapons were just as common as AK-47s and handguns. Moreover, relatively little is known about the types of strategies that armed groups used during this civil conflict. It is clear that brutalities such as amputation, burning houses, rape, and looting were commonplace. Women I interviewed also described unexpected or unique responsibilities during the war. For example, Mariatu was recruited by the AFRC/RUF as a military scout. When asked, "What were your role(s) during the conflict?" she answered, "To caress pro-government commanders and slowly kill them by excessive sex poisoning." Another former female soldier, Jeneba, spoke about the role of "witchcraft" or customary practices during war—particularly for the Kamajors. Jeneba explained that her role during the conflict was to "do concoctions and oracle activities in the holy shrine."[30] More research is needed to extend our understanding of the various types of roles, duties, and support that contributed to the civil conflict in Sierra Leone. These responses indicate that the types of contributions and warfare activities performed by men and women in Sierra Leone were diverse and complicated.

Third, this distinction is not helpful because most of the women I spoke with participated in multiple roles, and some operated both as armed combatants and in so-called support roles. For example, Amina was abducted by the SLA during the January rebel attack on the city.[31] She killed five people during her stay with the rebel forces and admitted to using a knife and a pistol. She also amputated the hands of a woman. While she was with the army, she also looted and destroyed property and worked as a cook and as a "sex slave."

In addition to performing multiple roles during the conflict, there is evidence from these interviews that contradicts the assumption that female combatants were a small minority within armed groups. Several interviewees reported that at different points in time women and girls were equal in numbers to men and may have even outnumbered men. For example, one interviewee reported that "sometimes there were more women than men and sometimes there were more men than women."[32] Tryphena, a woman who was a cook and a domestic worker for the RUF specified that she worked with at least fifty-five women. When Salamatu, a woman who was abducted by the rebel forces and later fought with them as a soldier, was asked how many other females were in her rebel group, she replied "many" and admitted that it would be difficult to know the exact number. She reported that she was abducted "at the time the amputations were on" and said "they amputated so many girls, others were killed. So the numbers become difficult to know, but there were many." Another respondent simply added that there were "many, many" women and girls from different factions and working under different commanders.

Zainab, a young female soldier and one of the few women interviewed who went through the DDR, reported participating in the war as a soldier for two years. Her reported activities included fighting and killing. Zainab reported that there were at least a hundred women fighting alongside her in her group and that "all had guns."[33] It is impossible to know exactly how many women and girl soldiers participated in the conflict in Sierra Leone; however, these interviews are significant in that they challenge existing perceptions of a civil war composed primarily of male soldiers and rebels, with female soldiers as rare minorities.

These interviews demonstrate the futility of binaries between "victims" of the war and perpetrators of violence, crime, and destruction. This is not exclusive to women and girls; there exist a great number of accounts of the war showing that most male soldiers were also victimized. For example, as mentioned in chapter 5, many males were forced to commit rape or to watch the rape of a family member. Also, a "recruitment" technique used by rebel forces for both males and females was to force recruits to kill a family member to prove their loyalty or reinforce their dependency on the armed movement. Most female soldiers I interviewed had experienced trauma or abuse *and* participated in some form of violent or destructive activity. In sum, these women were not *either* victims *or* combatants or *either* bush wives *or* soldiers; rather, they had diverse experiences and participated in various roles that blurred these distinct lines.

The stories of two female soldiers help illustrate this point. First, according to the child intake forms at CAW, Saphi was a former child soldier who arrived at a children's DDR facility with deep machete wounds on the side of her head. Saphi divulged that she was a child soldier with the SLA and that she killed, looted, partook in drug abuse, and was raped. She described how she came to be with the SLA: "I was abducted and forced to join, but if I resisted I would have been killed. In my presence my brother and friend were killed so I joined them." Second, when Fatima was found after the war, she knew her father was dead but did not know where her mother was or if she was alive. Fatima said that she had participated in "all major experiences" while with the RUF. She said she was a combatant fighter who had participated in killings, looted and destroyed property, and was "used for sex" by other rebels.

Beyond Followers and Sex Slaves: Engendering Representations

A variety of titles were constructed to avoid calling women and girls soldiers, including "camp followers," "abductees," "sex slaves," "domestic slaves," "girls and women associated with the fighting forces," and "vulnerable groups associated with armed movements." One of the facilitators of the DDR program admitted, "Women were just seen as camp followers even though some were active combatants and some went through military training."[34]

Rachel Brett is among those who have argued that disarmament organizers were unable to see past the participation of females in roles such as sex slaves, "wives," and domestic workers, to recognize their participation as combatants, killers, looters, and performers of amputations.[35] Similarly, focusing specifically on the disarmament process, Susan McKay and Dyan Mazurana argue that having "DDR processes planned and implemented by military officials has resulted in a bias against those the military does not consider 'real soldiers' (i.e. men with guns)."[36] Mazurana and Khristopher Carlson have also determined that in Sierra Leone there was an "over-classification of girls and young women abducted by the RUF, AFRC, and SLA as 'camp followers,' 'sex-slaves,' and 'wives' by some within the international community and the Sierra Leone government."[37]

In fact, even major international organizations that helped oversee the DDR process have been reluctant to name women and girls as combatants. The Girls Left Behind program, designed to benefit women and girls who should have been included in the DDR, makes little reference to the title "soldiers."[38] In an hour-long interview with Glenis Taylor, a senior director at UNICEF Sierra Leone, she never used the term "soldier" to refer to women and girls who fought and lived with armed groups. Instead, she identified them as "girls with the fighting forces" and "girls who were involved with the fighting forces."[39]

Original, unpublished correspondence I discovered at the offices of Children Associated with the War (CAW) demonstrates the reluctance of the Sierra Leone government to acknowledge female combatants. The below letter was written by CAW's director to the NCDDR, asking if some child soldiers could be retroactively included in the disarmament program. The following is an excerpt:

> We would be grateful if you could please facilitate the retroactive demobilization of child ex-combatants in the Peacock farm and Waterloo communities in the western area following an assessment carried out by the above program through its outreach program of activities. Discussions emanating from our assessment reveal that all of these children had left their guns and ammunition with their commanders in their various operational areas, but are resolved to settle down with their families and parents to rebuild their lives. It is therefore worth knowing that child combatants, particularly girls, are unwilling and most times reluctant to register with NCDDR due to social factors as they sneak into communities of origin without having gone through the DDR process. In this connection we forward a clear list of child ex-combatants that have been sensitized and have expressed their willingness to be formally registered with the DDR unit.[40]

It is important to note that CAW's records indicated that almost half the girls interviewed had participated in a variety of combat roles during the conflict. A selected review of the duties reported included killing and looting, being "introduced into the use of weapons and guns," possessing an AK-47, amputation, and using a knife and a pistol. The following reply from Dr. M. S. Tejan-kella, the disarmament and demobilization manager, to CAW's letter demonstrates that, despite evidence indicating that girls were active combatants, the NCDDR was unwilling to recognize them as such:

> Dear Sir,
> Regarding the retroactive demobilization of child ex combatants.
> I refer to your letter dated 1 March 2001, requesting for retroactive demobilization of child ex combatants of the Peacock farm and Waterloo rural communities. I wish to inform you that DDR cannot retroactively demobilize these children as they have proved to be camp followers and

abductees and not combatants. We regret any inconvenience this decision may cause.

Children Associated with the War retained all the intake forms for child soldiers, abducted children, and unaccompanied children who were brought to its centers over the course of the war. It was unclear what distinguished "unaccompanied children" from "abducted children" and "child soldiers" because most children had similar stories and had participated in similar activities during the war. Both "abandoned children" and "unaccompanied children" seemed to be defined in relation to their disassociation from the family unit. These categories imply that the children were abandoned or left unaccompanied by family members. As such, the two categories of children are seen as problematic not because of their experiences or roles during the war but because of this separation from the family unit. Most "unaccompanied children" were girls.

Interestingly, the majority of the unaccompanied girls reported working with or for the armed groups in some capacity. Most worked as cooks, and almost all listed one of their "noncombatant" duties as "sex service." This information further complicates the distinctions between combatant, noncombatant, and "supporter." Clearly these girls were doing work that helped sustain the armed movement. Further analysis of the distinctions that were made not only between combatant and supporter but also between particular forms of labor is required. A gendered hierarchy seems to exist whereby "masculine" or male-dominated roles such as carrying arms and looting property is prioritized over domestic forms of labor such as cooking. Furthermore, there has been little analysis of how sex slavery was used as a means to enhance troop morale and thereby sustain armed conflict. If sex and rape were central to compensating and motivating male soldiers, it cannot continue to be classified as irrelevant with reference to soldiering activities. Data from the intake forms for several of the girls identified as unaccompanied children are included here to help illustrate these points:[41]

> Esther arrived at CAW at the age of sixteen with a bullet wound on her left foot. Both of her parents were reported dead. Esther told social workers, "I was abducted by the RUF and was taken away. I was a cook and also raped each and every day. I witnessed a lot of horrible things like killing, maiming, and beheading of innocent civilians." During the eight months

she was with the RUF, her "noncombatant roles" included acting as a gun carrier and a cook and performing sexual services.

Lovetta was sixteen and had no disabilities at the time she was brought to CAW. She was in school before the war, and her parents were thought to be alive. She told social workers, "I was caught between the crossfire during the January invasion and was taken away by Captain Armstrong of SLA. There I came to identify a group called the small boys club, since I was taking care of the food and belongings." She was with the SLA for ten months, recruited at fifteen. On the intake form her "noncombatant roles" were listed as "cook" and "sex service." The final section of the form notes that Lovetta looted, was raped, and partook in drug abuse.

Fea was sixteen when she arrived at CAW. It is reported that "she came impregnated from the bush" and "she's not well." Fea explained to CAW social workers that she was operating a small business before the war. The social workers recorded the following details about Fea: "She was abducted by the AFRC/RUF rebels during their retreat from the city under heavy ECOMOG guns." Fea told social workers that her mother is dead and her father is alive. Her "noncombatant roles" were listed as "cook" and "sex service." Fea answered yes to both of the following questions: Did you rape? Were you raped?

Isatu arrived at CAW with fragments of an unknown material in her left hand. She was seventeen. Isatu knew that her father was dead but believed her mother was still alive. Isatu described how her mother fell ill during the war, and Isatu was forced to find medicine for her. While looking for medicine she was caught by the SLA and was "seriously sexually harassed." She stayed with the SLA for nine months. Her "noncombatant roles" were loading guns, carrying supplies, cooking, and performing sexual services.

Social workers at CAW noted of Salamatu, a seventeen-year-old girl, that "she looks well." She worked as a tailor before the war, and her parents were thought to be alive. She gave the following account of her capture into the RUF: "When the rebels attacked mile 91 with heavy firing we were compelled to escape but were later captured by the RUF. I was abducted at the same time I saw the killings of people. My children were sick in the bush." Like many of the female unaccompanied children, Salamatu's "noncombatant roles" were listed as "cook" and "sex service." She also reported being raped while with the rebels.

Marie was also seventeen when she reported to CAW. She was reported to be anemic, and social workers recorded that she "doesn't look well." Marie described her abduction by the RUF: "I was abducted while trying to escape from the rebels at one of the hospitals since I was sick." She also noted that she "cooked for the combatants" and "saw killings being done."

Fatmata is a seventeen-year-old who arrived at CAW with bullet wounds on her left leg. She was abducted by the SLA during the January rebel incursion into Freetown and remained with them for nine months. She noted that she had been raped by a famous commander called Rambo and added that she experienced pains after being raped. Fatmata also witnessed two rapists killed before her. Her "noncombatant roles" were documented as "cook" and "sex service."

Kadiatu was only nine years old when she was taken to CAW. She told social workers she did not know where her parents were and that she was abducted by the RUF "when they attacked Kono." Kadiatu was with the RUF for one year and eight months. During that time her "noncombatant roles" included fetching water, making beds, and assisting in cooking.

Mabintu was nicknamed "bad girl." At seventeen, she arrived at CAW with no injuries or disabilities. She gave the following account of her time with the RUF forces: "I was captured when I on holiday to [see] my mother. After that I became a maid servant to a female commander, a Liberian.... I witnessed so many atrocities like the extraction of human heart after they had been killed." She was with the RUF for four years and ten months before she escaped. Her "noncombatant roles" included acting as a maid and looting. She reported that she did not know where her mother was, but that she knew her father and her uncle were dead.

This information indicates that most unaccompanied girls worked in some capacity for armed movements and therefore should be classified as soldiers. This information confirms the argument that women and girl soldiers were reclassified into various categories distinguished by their vulnerability. There is no doubt that girl soldiers—and boy soldiers—were vulnerable and faced serious risks during and after the war; however, categorizing girls as "unaccompanied children" rather than soldiers obscures their contribution to the conflict. Not only were their contributions to the conflict ignored, but girls were denied the post-conflict resources and attention directed at other former child soldiers. A great deal of resources were directed toward child soldiers post-conflict; therefore, those children who were classified as unaccompanied children were disadvantaged because they were not eligible for the same reintegration opportunities as child soldiers.

The Consequences of Losing the Soldier Title

The manner in which male and female soldiers have been categorized post–armed conflict has had several interrelated impacts: first, stripping women and girls of their titles as soldiers by distinguishing them from "true" or "real" combatants depoliticized their roles during the conflict; second, as development grows ever more concerned with people and issues identified as security concerns, depoliticizing the role of women and girls during the conflict meant that they were not targeted as primary beneficiaries for post-conflict programs and reintegration initiatives; third, deprioritizing and depoliticizing females has meant that the reintegration process for them has largely been seen as a social rather than a political process, a "returning to normal" that would happen naturally, or at least privately. In effect, this categorization removes women and girls from policy discourses, absolves policy makers from addressing them as a category, and reinforces gendered assumptions about acceptable and normal roles in conflict.

In post-conflict Sierra Leone, international organizations, NGOs, and aid agencies have funding, networks, and influence that garner them significant positions of power in comparison to Sierra Leone's shaky government. As a result, these organizations possess the ability to selectively securitize issues and determine their priority. Given the radicalization of development, or the increasing attention to security as a major factor in development, NGOs and aid agencies have a particular stake in designating a societal phenomenon a security concern requiring immediate attention. Due to the escalating emphasis placed on security by development actors and governments, securitizing an issue is an effective method for garnering funding; it indicates that an urgent response is required and that addressing this particular issue is central to stability and peace.

The radicalization of development in Sierra Leone has meant that issues understood as traditional security concerns, including disarmament, unemployed men, and male soldiers, have been given significant attention in the post-conflict context. Moreover, matters relating to women, including sexual violence and female soldiers, continue to be categorized as domestic, social, or private matters. Male soldiers continue to be securitized post-conflict, in contrast to the "naturalization" and domestication of women. Post-conflict programs that assume women and girls are victims lacking agency have dismissed, isolated, and silenced a vast cohort of women and girls.

Conclusion

The Copenhagen school describes security as a political category resulting in the prioritization of particular issues or events as significant over "everyday politics." In the case of post–armed conflict Sierra Leone, one of the political forces operating on the selection of security concerns is gender. In this case male former combatants are securitized while female former combatants are marginalized. The reluctance by international aid agencies, the United Nations, the World Bank, and other international organizations to name female soldiers as soldiers rather than "females associated with the war," "dependents," or "camp followers" ignores and depoliticizes their roles during the conflict. In addition, this construction relegates them spatially to the private realm—well away from the attention given to securitized and politicized matters.

The relationship between notions of "stability," "peace," "victim" and "violent," "threatening," "conflict" to presumptions about femininity and masculinity must be unpacked in order to illustrate how security discourses not only continue to discount the role of women and girls in otherwise securitized activities but also contribute to the reconstruction of "normal" female subjects as benevolent, nurturing, or victims in contrast to violent and aggressive males. Women and girls have been victimized during conflict; however, they have participated in violence out of coercion and, in some cases, out of choice.

What this analysis does make clear is that the time has come that the voluntary participation of women and girls in traditionally male dominated activities such as war can no longer be overlooked. In Sierra Leone, the effectiveness of post–armed conflict programming, an inclusive transition from conflict to peace, and gender equality post–armed conflict have been compromised because of this omission—an error that will be repeated so long as reconstruction programs remain blind to the needs of women not only as victims but as participants in conflicts around the world.

4

Empowerment Boom or Bust?

Assessing Women's Post–Armed Conflict Empowerment Initiatives

As a member of the Revolutionary United Front, Kadie took part in the amputation of civilians, looted and burned property, and was subjected to multiple sexual abuses. Although she went through the DDR process in Sierra Leone, Kadie complained that the program "ended too quickly" and did not provide her with the skills or the resources that were initially promised. She recounted how pro-government forces were given priority whereas antigovernment forces were discriminated against within the DDR process. She admitted that she knew little about the process in general and felt that most of the information about it was not successfully made public. She called the program "a lie" and felt that its resources had been "directed to particular political groups." She described her current situation as "frustrating" because she felt she was "economically and socially poor" and faced public stigma and ridicule as a result of her soldier status. She described women's situation in Sierra Leone generally as desperately unequal. She reported that women are "treated with gross exclusion in decision making" and in "all aspects" of development. Kadie recommended that the program should have included education for women soldiers.

"Empowerment" has become one of the most frequently used terms in development discourses today. From the creation of water wells to microfinance programs to political awareness campaigns, development initiatives have lauded themselves as sources of empowerment for their beneficiaries. As with many other buzzwords in development, actors offer vastly disparate, and often vague, definitions of empowerment. Despite the varying conceptions of the term, empowerment is consistently associated with progressive, representative, and inclusive development policies and programs. Specifically, for many development actors, empowerment programs are advertised as proof that development approaches have evolved in response to previous criticisms of the top-down, centralized nature of such initiatives. Empowerment is meant to signal the new face of development, one that is driven by local interests, concerned with individual concerns, and representative of community needs.

Women's empowerment in particular has become a stated goal for several major development actors, including the United Nations, the World Bank, the Organization for Economic Cooperation and Development (OECD), and a host of NGOs. Despite the empowerment boom within development, there has been little systematic analysis of possible cross-cutting themes of empowerment initiatives, the roots of empowerment discourses, or the extent to which empowerment programs indeed exhibit a shift toward more representative, inclusive, and localized development approaches.[1] In particular, for decades feminist and postcolonial scholars have been advocating for the type of marked transformation of development methods that empowerment projects claim to provide, yet there remains a need for rigorous analysis of specific women's empowerment programs.

Using reintegration programs for female soldiers in Sierra Leone as a case study, it is argued here that neoliberal ideals such as individualism, responsibility, and economic discipline have shaped empowerment initiatives to a far greater extent than considerations of local input, marginalized groups, or representation. Moreover, instead of representing a shift in development approaches, projects advertising themselves as sources of women's empowerment—including the reintegration process in Sierra Leone—are informed by liberal understandings of conjugal order and serve to discipline subjects with explicit messages about appropriate gendered social order and legitimate behaviors.

This argument is explored through a brief review of the emergence of empowerment as a central concept within dominant approaches to development. Next, the disarmament, demobilization, and reintegration process—particularly the reintegration portion—will be considered as an example of programs claiming to empower beneficiaries. An explanation of the DDR process in Sierra Leone will be provided and followed by a focus on the reintegration process for female soldiers. Following this description, several concerns with the organization and implementation of the DDR will be addressed. This critique is based on interview data with several Sierra Leoneans who either worked for the DDR or worked in other forms of post–armed conflict reintegration initiatives. Finally, female soldiers' own reactions and evaluations of the reintegration process are presented.

This chapter points to broader issues surrounding neoliberal, largely Western-led development. First, it builds on the critical work of scholars such as Uma Kothari and Bill Cooke, who have pointed to development discourses as a source of reincarnation for development actors whose priorities are to gain power, stay in business, and institute a particular social, political, and gender order.[2] Second, it addresses the tension between critical, alternative, and truly local visions of development and the hegemonic status of neoliberal development with its emphasis on economic openness, individualism, and productivity. Third—inspired by the work of feminist scholars such as Christine Sylvester, Laura Sjoberg, and Cynthia Enloe—this chapter reveals how embedded notions of conjugal order and gendered norms are within Western-led development as well as the hypermasculine nature both of conflict and of post-conflict reconstruction and peacekeeping.[3]

Cynthia Cockburn has argued that there are two schools of thought in peace and post-conflict studies: those who "stand above conflict and look for rational value-free solutions" and those who "take issue" with notions of neutrality in post-conflict reconstruction.[4] This chapter is inspired by the latter premise. The aim of highlighting these wider concerns is not to convince the reader that all is lost; rather, the objective is to make the case that making slight adjustments to conventional development models or framing old policies with new discourses is not enough. Gender hierarchies and norms are deeply ingrained within dominant approaches to development; therefore, discursive dodges or shifts cannot replace radical critique and reform.

Approach

This chapter develops the argument that development policies serve as a source of regulation and discipline. Drawing from Foucault's and Hansen's work on discourse and discipline, this chapter is focused on the language of post-conflict development policies in Sierra Leone and the power relationships and norms that are instituted and regulated by these policies. In addition, Jacqueline Stevens's work on the phenomenology of the natural is utilized to help understand the specific gendered power dynamics associated with post-conflict policy making and the significance of conjugal order to notions of social order and peace. As mentioned earlier, Stevens argues that normalizing or making the nuclear family seem natural renders the family as "impervious," prepolitical, and "immutable."[5] From Stevens's analysis, it becomes worthwhile to reconsider representations of the nuclear family unit specifically and conjugal order more broadly within development policy discourses as natural and prepolitical. Depicting the family and conjugal order in this manner implies that a whole set of gendered norms and relationships are necessary, unchanging, and outside the realm of political intervention.

With an emphasis on women, this chapter is also critical of development programs that claim to represent marginalized groups. Specifically, the trend within empowerment initiatives to emphasize "local," "indigenous," or "community" knowledge must be scrutinized. Here, Uma Kothari's critical work on development policy is especially relevant.[6] Kothari points out that development actors construct notions of the "local" and represent similar terms within their policies as if they were a fixed entity. In turn, she argues that although policies purporting to represent the local or the grassroots appear to be inclusive, more often, notions of grassroots, local, and indigenous are constructed in ways that legitimize existing Western-liberal development policies and solidify the role of outside development actors.[7]

Given the growing number of policies claiming to be representative of women, gender inclusive, and a source of women's empowerment, it is crucial to investigate the motivations of these policies, what efforts have been made to represent women's needs, and what sorts of gender norms and stereotypes might be implied through these policies. Feminist theorists—particularly those who emphasize language and discourse—have argued that women's ability to speak for themselves, to describe their own needs and their own objectives, and, most important, to have their voices heard is paramount to women's empowerment.[8] From this perspective, there is much at stake if empowerment initiatives that emphasize responsibility, economic progress, self-determination, and individual liability are largely void of women's individual voices, individual accounts, or even community consultations.

Similar to the other chapters in this volume, this chapter focuses on representation and discourse; thus, discourse analysis is employed. The focus of the discourse analysis includes a brief genealogy of the growth of the use of empowerment and women's empowerment in development policy discourses. This is followed by an analysis of the manner in which the DDR in Sierra Leone was framed as a source of empowerment—especially for women. Throughout a review of the reintegration process for women, neoliberal themes and approaches are highlighted. A more general analysis of the reintegration process in Sierra Leone and the power dynamics associated with reintegration policies as well as the manner in which these policies construct female soldiers, constrain their behavior, and recast appropriate social roles for women is also presented. Interview data are then contrasted to representations of the reintegration process as a source of empowerment for women.

Empowerment and Development

Over the last decade perhaps no term has been both as generously employed and as woefully ill-defined as "empowerment." In particular, women's empowerment has been embraced by such a vast number of development actors that it appears to be a unifying mission within development. For example, the OECD has stated that "investment in gender equity and women's empowerment is vital for improving economic political and social conditions in developing countries within the framework of sustainable development," and "a focus on gender equality and women's empowerment is a means to enhance the total effectiveness of aid."[9] Similarly, the UN has identified women's advancement and empowerment in decision making as an essential element of sustainable development.[10] The empowerment of people, specifically women, was also announced as the main objective of development at the Copenhagen Declaration of the World Summit on Social Development. The UN recognized women's empowerment and gender equality as a Millennium Development Goal "in their own right and central to all other development efforts."[11] The United Nations Development Program (UNDP) has also categorized women's empowerment as a major policy goal. UNDP policies related to women's empowerment tend to emphasize individual participation, skills, and economic self-reliance.[12] Perhaps most significant is the addition of the Gender Empowerment Measure and the Gender-Related Development Index to the United Nations Human Development Index rankings.

In both general empowerment initiatives and women's empowerment programs, the influence of neoliberalism is evident. Several of the themes linking empowerment approaches include an emphasis on the individual; economic independence as a major objective; and the focus on economic responsibility, capacity enhancement, choice, and productivity. For example, the World Bank defines "empowerment" as "the process of increasing the *capacity* of individuals or groups to make *choices* and to transform those choices into desired actions and outcomes. Central to this process are actions that both build individual and collective assets, and improve the *efficiency* and fairness of the organizational and institutional contexts which govern the use of these assets."[13] Similarly, although the OECD does not explicitly define "empowerment," the term is frequently linked to other terms such as "local," "equality," "effectiveness," "self-help," "capacity-building," and "decentralization."[14] In addition, the United Nations Population Fund (UNFPA) recognizes economic empowerment—particularly microfinance—as a central approach to empowering women.

Background

After the signing of the Lomé Peace Accord in 1999, international organizations and development institutions began implementing a variety of peace, development, and reconstruction programs. In particular, the DDR was initiated to help former soldiers make the transition to citizens. Following Sierra Leone's conflict, nearly 75,000 soldiers were received at more than seventy centers for disarmament.[15] The reintegration phases of the program for adults and children officially ended in 2002 and 2005, respectively; however, there is evidence that frontline workers and citizens of Sierra Leone still feel reintegration and rehabilitation are not complete.[16]

Numerous sources have described the disarmament process as a key element for achieving security and sustainable peace. Specifically, the DDR program in Sierra Leone was touted as a fundamental element of the country's transition out of civil conflict.[17] I argue that the DDR is a prime example of Mark Duffield's account of the radicalization of development, or the coalescence of development and security policies.[18] The three phases of the DDR were designed with the understanding that peace will not result merely from the removal of guns from the hands of combatants; rather, a regimented process of rehabilitation and societal reconstruction is a prerequisite for a secure nation.

In the middle of 1998, in the midst of continued violence and insecurity, the government of Sierra Leone announced it had designed a plan for national disarmament. The Sierra Leone government and the World Bank established the Multi-Donor Trust Fund (MDTF) to solicit funding from the international donor community for the DDR, with the World Bank, UNICEF, the United Nations Mission in Sierra Leone (UNAMSIL), and the Sierra Leone government providing a significant portion of the funding. The National Committee for Disarmament, Demobilization and Reintegration was created to oversee the three-phase process of disarmament, demobilization, and reintegration. One of the central objectives of the DDR was to "support the short term economic and social reintegration of eligible ex-combatants."[19] The initial mandate was to target 45,000 soldiers from the RUF, the CDF, and the SLA; by the time the program finished its mandate in 2002, however, some 75,000 combatants had been disarmed at approximately seventeen demobilization centers around the country.

Disarmament, Demobilization, and Reintegration

The government of Sierra Leone defined disarmament as the "voluntary laying down of all weapons and ammunition by all warring parties for lasting peace in Sierra Leone."[20] After the establishment of the United Nations Observer Mission in Sierra Leone (UNOMSIL) in July 1998, one of this organization's primary mandates was the monitoring of the disarmament and demobilization of ex-combatants. Especially after periods of humiliation for the UN missions in Sierra Leone at the expense of armed groups, the disarmament of combatants in Sierra Leone became tied to the perceived success of UNOMSIL and later UNAMSIL.[21] Essentially, the disarmament phase involved the handing over of weapons by ex-combatants to UN officials.

Demobilization typically involves two stages—the processing of former soldiers and the distribution of support packages or financial assistance to assist soldiers in moving toward the reintegration process. Demobilization centers were established throughout Sierra Leone, and ex-combatants were housed there for periods ranging from two to ninety days. This range was largely a result of inconsistent funding and the impact of renewed hostilities.[22] At demobilization centers, ex-combatants were given food, water, and shelter while information was collected about their involvement in the conflict and they were administered through a national identification process. Ex-combatants were given photo ID cards that were required for reintegration activities; in effect, ex-combatants had to participate in the entire demobilization process to be eligible for training and education opportunities. The demobilization process was declared over in February 2002, one month after the disarmament phase ended.

According to the NCDDR, Sierra Leone's government body directing the process, the reintegration phase of the DDR was designed to support "the social and economic reintegration of ex-combatants by engaging them in productive activities beneficial to them and facilitating their return to their families and communities."[23] The goal of reintegration programs was to facilitate the ex-combatants' social and economic reintegration into communities so that they might "participate fully in all traditional and social events in the communities without inhibitions."[24] The NCDDR described their efforts in the reintegration phase of the DDR as "support" to ex-combatants for "their resettlement into normal society."[25] There were a variety of "sensitization" campaigns to encourage communities and families to accept former combatants into their homes and communities. However, the bulk of reintegration activities focused on training and education for ex-combatants. Depending on their age and education level, ex-combatants were given the choice of formal education, vocational and skills training, an apprentice opportunity, or a public works/job placement option.

Reintegration programs in Sierra Leone were generally focused on providing skills training for ex-combatants. As mentioned in chapter 2, vocational skills were offered in the following areas: carpentry, metalworking, auto mechanics, tailoring, *gara* tie-dyeing, soap making, hairdressing, plumbing and masonry, electrical work, computer skills, building material production, and basic construction and technology. Training lasted between three and nine months, depending on the trade. The apprentice program offered similar trades and was designed for those with limited education. According to NCDDR statistics, 39 percent of ex-combatants chose formal education, 23 percent chose skills training, 10 percent chose an apprenticeship, and approximately 4 percent chose public works and job placement.[26] In addition, 2,385 former RUF and CDF soldiers were recruited into the Sierra Leone Army.[27]

Empowerment and Reintegration

The DDR is an example of programs that advertise themselves as sources of empowerment in post-conflict situations. The UN has been a major donor to DDR processes around the world, including in Sierra Leone. In 2006 the UN released a comprehensive overview of the DDR process, including lessons learned and guiding principles of DDR. In this report, empowerment is listed as a major objective of the DDR and a direct product of capacity-building—one of the guiding principles of the report. In addition, "support to local capacity development and community empowerment" is identified by the UN as a key area of national support associated with the DDR.[28] More specifically, women's empowerment has been described as integral to gender mainstreaming DDR programs.[29]

In the case of Sierra Leone, empowerment was emphasized as an objective of the DDR. Before the conflict had officially ended, Francis Kai-Kai, the executive secretary of the NCDDR in Sierra Leone, described youth empowerment as a part of the peace and reconciliation process.[30] In Sierra Leone, stakeholders also described the reintegration phase of the DDR as the process whereby soldiers were stripped of their power as soldiers and "empowered" as valued citizens of the post-conflict community.[31]

There are numerous indicators of neoliberal influences in terms of the way empowerment was used in reference to the reintegration process in Sierra Leone. In particular, reintegration programs focused mainly on economic productivity. For example, the U.S. Agency for International Development (USAID) declared that it would help to empower citizens of Sierra Leone "in part by helping them build effective links among local councils, traditional, and national leaders, to broaden and strengthen the voice of the people."[32] However, when referring to reintegration activities, USAID narrowed its focus to "providing ex-combatants and war-affected youth with job skills and income earning opportunities."[33] USAID is also careful to mention the importance of individuals, choice, and capacity:

> USAID's democracy program in Sierra Leone equips local people, including women and youth, with the information and skills they need to participate in decision-making, tackle corruption, and contain human rights abuses with a view to end the cycle of violence and ensure security and stability.[34]

There are certainly other key terms within reintegration programs and policies in Sierra Leone that mirror broader trends in empowerment discourses. The reintegration process was lauded as a grassroots initiative directed by communities and representative of the variety of actors involved in the conflict. Phrases and words like "bottom-up," "grassroots," and "local knowledge," as well as "productivity," "efficiency," and "individual responsibility" are rife within reintegration program documents in Sierra Leone. Initial planning for reintegration programs seemed to have avoided "top-down" bureaucratic development processes. For example, the Child Protection Committees of Sierra Leone published a paper in 1998 declaring that psychosocial reintegration initiatives for child soldiers would "be adapted to local economic realities and realities and will follow as much as possible the individual interest."[35] The following was also specified in the report:

> Preference must be given to traditional occupations related to local markets and socioeconomic reality. Projects must encourage using local skills and techniques based on traditional and customary knowledge that may be improved with external support. Likewise, if vocational training programs are launched, they should be based on market assessments.[36]

In contrast, and as will be elaborated further, the implementation of the DDR was remarkably centralized and placed significant emphasis on neoliberal notions of individualism, responsibility, and economic progress. One theme of reintegration was described as "preparation of and support for former combatants in their socio-economic reinsertion and reintegration after leaving the demobilization centers."[37] The UN reported that through income-generating activities, "youth dropouts and ex-combatants will be encouraged to participate in order to redirect their energies and talents to productive pursuits."[38]

Reintegration for Female Soldiers

As already noted, the majority of female soldiers did not participate in the DDR, and women made up a very small number of the total population of disarmed soldiers in Sierra Leone. For those females who did participate, the DDR process was markedly different than for males. First, the training options available to women were highly limited, with *gara* tie-dyeing, soap making, tailoring, catering, hairdressing, and weaving as the main choices for skills training. The few reintegration programs targeting female soldiers consistently offered these same select trades. For example, UNICEF's Girls Left Behind program—an initiative directed specifically toward females—offered training in *gara* tie-dyeing, catering, tailoring, and weaving. Other local and international organizations offered the same limited training choices for female ex-combatants.

In fact, two local organizations focusing on female ex-soldiers—Children Associated with the War and the Augustan Bintue organization—had only tailoring available as a training option. These training options were limiting primarily because they tended to be more popular in rural regions and were far less lucrative than options available to males. In fact, because so many females were trained in these few trades, some communities had an overabundance of *gara* tie-dyers or soap makers, rendering the skills nearly useless.[39] These options were highly gendered and were ineffectual because they were not chosen in consultation with communities or female beneficiaries.

The trades offered to female soldiers were chosen by the NCDDR, which was advised by the World Bank, the UN, UNICEF, and other international organizations. A local market assessment was never undertaken to determine whether these trades would be useful for women and girls or for communities more broadly. When program coordinators were asked about the relevance of the trades for women, most simply replied that their organizations only received funding to offer those specific trades.[40] Therefore, if a community organization had decided to offer basic education or skills training in another area, it would not have received funding. Other options for female soldiers included special programs created for groups identified by the NCDDR as "particularly vulnerable post conflict," including child ex-combatants, disabled ex-combatants, and female ex-combatants.[41] Within this category, programs for female ex-combatants were described by the NCDDR as "family stabilization measures" and primarily featured microcredit initiatives. The stated objective of these programs was "to provide financial support to ex-combatant families . . . in order to reduce family pressures on male ex-combatants."[42]

Reordering, Not Reintegrating

For Sierra Leone, the function of the development community in reshaping gender roles during the reintegration process cannot be overlooked. Organizations in Sierra Leone largely treated the reintegration of women and girls as a social process, a returning to normal that would either happen naturally, with time, or through sensitization—meaning talking to communities and families about the need to take women and girls back. In particular, there was great concern about the marriageability of female soldiers largely because it was assumed they had been raped or had given birth to children out of wedlock.[43] In some cases, grandmothers offered to raise the children of former soldiers so they could marry without men having to worry about supporting "rebel children."[44] Some organizations even encouraged former female soldiers to marry their rape perpetrators to avoid shame and to blend into the community.[45]

Women were given few choices in their reintegration process: silence or stigma, limited training or nothing, isolation or marriage, stigma or motherhood, ostracism or returning to their families. Each of these choices was seen as an opportunity to hide their identities as soldiers and to "blend in" "naturally" to the community and family unit. Jaqueline Stevens argues, "To 'naturalize' is to express the necessity of a form of being or practice, to make something seem impervious to human intention and immutable."[46] Understood this way, naturalizing the process of reintegration for women and girls in Sierra Leone effectively desecuritized female soldiers and justified the limited attention given to them. By encouraging women and girl soldiers to return to their "normal places" in the community, any new roles or positions of authority they may have held during the conflict are stripped from them, and any opportunities to rethink and reshape gender stereotypes and hierarchies are destroyed.

Normal women become defined primarily as victims of the war while women and girls who were soldiers, who were perpetrators of violence and destruction, who volunteered to participate in conflict, or who were empowered by the conflict become categorized as deviants. Lene Hansen posits that "the positive value ascribed to 'women' is preconditioned upon women's acceptance of the subject position bestowed upon them. If 'women' were to be constructed, or construct themselves, as less motherly, less caring, and less publicly passive, their supplementary privilege would in all likelihood be suspended."[47] Post-conflict conjugal order in Sierra Leone reinforced age-old stereotypes about peaceful women and the natural place for women in society, thereby erasing violent women and girls as legitimate subjects. Thus, for women and girls, the return to normal entailed conforming to, and participating in, a distinct form of conjugal order; the return to normal also involved a process of denying or hiding any activities, desires, or plans that did not conform to perceptions of conjugal order.

Problems with Programs from an Organizational Viewpoint

Many local experts I spoke with in Sierra Leone were quick to point out the weaknesses in the DDR program—particularly in terms of its ability to empower women. The two main limitations mentioned related to the skills training portion of the program and the manner in which women and girls were included in or excluded from the DDR. In terms of skills training, one of the weaknesses identified was the fact that there were very few options for ex-combatants to choose from. Not every reintegration program for women offered each of these trades; many organizations offered training in only one of these options. For example, former girl soldiers enrolled in CAW's reintegration initiative had one option—tailoring. The small number of trades often meant that there was an overabundance of women trained in specific areas, thereby diluting the marketability and worth of their trade. Small communities like Makeni, in central Sierra Leone, for example, might graduate a hundred females from training in *gara* tie-dyeing. If even half of them want to remain in the community, they will be competing with fifty other women trained in the same skill.

This leads to a second concern with the training options, which was that little research was done to determine the regional or local appropriateness, usefulness, or market demands for the skills. Sulay Sesay, a coordinator for the DDR, admitted that although a market assessment would have been useful in determining more appropriate and lucrative trades for women, this was never conducted: "At some point we thought we should have done a market survey of some of those trades we had chose[n]. . . . Then we realized that after training the opportunities for income generation were too few."[48]

Another criticism of reintegration programs was related to the length of time they were offered. When the DDR was first established, several reintegration training options were meant to be offered for a year. Later this was cut to nine months, then to six months. In the final stages of the disarmament process, some training programs were offered for a mere six weeks due to a shortage in funds and pressure from donor organizations to wrap up the process.

Both Glenis Taylor, a director at UNICEF Sierra Leone, and Abu Bakar Sesay, a social worker in Makeni, noted that a few years after the peace agreement was signed in Sierra Leone they were compelled by their donors to begin concluding their war-related reintegration programs regardless of whether there was still demand for these initiatives. Abu J. Conte, a program manager for child protection services in Makeni, noted that most of the child protection programs he was associated with were funded as "post-conflict" emergency initiatives and that current programs had to be reframed to donors as development activities: "We were working on a range of child protection actions—the DDR, interim care centers. But all those were within the context of emergency phase, now we are moving from emergency phase to developmental phase." Glenis Taylor also reported that her office was under pressure to alter its programming: "[Donors] are now saying that the war is over ... it is now five years since it is over ... it is now time to move away from [any] war associations."

Abu J. Conte and other local experts noted that this shift did not reflect reality on the ground as many of the "emergency" programs were still in process and/or were still necessary. For example, near the end of the children's disarmament process in 2005, Abu Bakar Sesay noted, "The community reintegration program is over this December and there are still children that need the education. So for many children their education will end. It is very sad. It offloads the responsibility for school fees to the parents and people can't afford it."

Local experts like Edward Anague (director of CEDA, an organization focused on inclusive approaches to post-conflict reconstruction) and Rev. Hassan Mansaray (director of Children Integrated Services [CIS], an organization working with war-affected children) argued that abbreviating the training programs resulted in several undesirable outcomes. First, former soldiers were not sufficiently adept at their trade and were unable to support themselves with the limited skills passed on to them. Anague explained that former soldiers

> need something that creates employment for themselves. If you train [an ex-combatant] for only 6 months she can't even fix a button. What can you call that person? Not a seamstress.... You need to change [sic] by removing the person from the horrible environment and give them something meaningful so that the person can see it as a legitimate option. It is a long-term process. It is not a crash course. It is not about $1,000 given to ex-combatants. If you want results it has to be more than a six-month program. NGOs and organizations are pressured to produce "results" [by donors], but it doesn't amount to anything.

Without skills training that has value in communities, former soldiers are forced to find alternatives for survival. In impoverished and war-torn communities, these options are limited. As Anague concluded, female ex-combatants need to know that they have a future in a particular trade, otherwise they will "turn their backs" on work and turn to something more lucrative such as prostitution.[49] He lamented that "some of the training was a waste of time for the ex-combatants. Before they even start the training they have to be comfortable and know that their future rests on the training they will receive. Some of them...they can make more money as sex slaves." Isha Kamara, a social worker who has worked with former female soldiers for years, confirmed that a large number of these women and girls are "roaming about the streets" because of lack of opportunities and that many turn to prostitution for survival.[50]

As mentioned earlier, DDR was meant to be a key element in ensuring that ex-combatants find alternative sources of income and ways of contributing to their community so that they would not take up arms again. The failure to offer training programs that fully prepared ex-combatants to sustain themselves economically resulted in ex-combatants returning to communities with no viable source of income and perhaps disappointed or disillusioned with the promises made by the local government and the international community regarding their reintegration. Thus, the prospect for long-term peace is called into question if the DDR did not even prepare soldiers for basic trades. Anague gave his perspective on the inadequacies of the reintegration process and warned of the potential dismal long-term consequences:

> I thought it [the DDR] was staying for ten years...it should have been a long process. When you have war for eleven years you need twenty-two years to reverse that. This is 2005, things take time to get back. The gun is under the table, it has not been destroyed. The people who will take the gun out are the neglected ex-combatants who have been neglected and who have been used to living by the gun. They feel deceived, maltreated, targeted. If you want to reform a person...you need to reform all because it is these neglected people who will take up arms again and reproduce children who will be raised to learn that war is the answer.

In addition to problems with the structure and focus, reintegration programs were criticized more generally for failing both to attract women and girls and to address their reintegration needs. Mameh Kargbo, a staff member of Cooperazeone Internazionale (COOPI), described the DDR as prohibitive to women and girls. She argued that the low number of women and girls who participated in the DDR was due to "oversight" and "the gender aspect of it." She gave the following account of the DDR:

> The mandate didn't spell "men only," but here in Sierra Leone we have a gender problem, you know, boys have more access to resources that will help them to excel than girls. So in institutions where they just leave things open the boys will grab most of the things...the structure made was mainly for men. One of the criteria was to go with guns—many of the girls were pregnant, and you have the culture where girls are not expected to be in that situation and so they find it difficult to show up. The sensitization was not much [to allow] for girls to show up. The DDR was mainly a male issue. The reason why the girls didn't come through...had to do with culture, some were pregnant, some had babies, and the perception of the DDR as a man issue. There was little sensitization that girls should have come too.

Kargbo went on to say that most pregnant women who presented themselves at the DDR were turned away and sent to humanitarian organizations like his.

Glenis Taylor from UNICEF admitted that during the planning stages of the DDR for children "the focus was just making sure that children were protected through the process—we weren't paying particular attention to the girls and their needs. That was a lesson learned looking back. We realized that there was not enough attention—at the time of planning we didn't think about all these needs." She went on to report that

> the demobilization process was mostly done by men. In fact some of the girls were deliberately given the wrong information about the DDR. For the children you didn't need a gun to demobilize—you just had to walk up. But some of them didn't know that, they thought you had to have a weapon. For some, the commanders deliberately kept [girls] in the dark because they didn't want to lose them.

Abu J. Conte noted another consequence of a gender-blind DDR. He commented on the problems associated with having a single demobilization center for both men and women as well as the proximity of adult demobilization centers to child demobilization centers. He described this as a particular problem for young women and girls. He explained, "There was a problem in keeping the girls in the demobilization camp. There were men coming and saying these were their wives and they want to take them out of the camps. For future programs, we recommend keeping a reasonable distance [between these groups]." Francis Lahai, the focal point for the Street Children's Task Force in Freetown, reached similar conclusions about the inadequacies of the DDR in meeting the specific needs of women and girls. Speaking specifically about disarmament for children, he recommended:

> For any organization wanting to replicate the DDR in Sierra Leone, they should not only target those child combatants that go for disarmament. There are many more that still remain and due to circumstances are unable to come for disarmament. They could check within households of commanders and those who were trapped in sexual relationships. Otherwise they are leaving a large number of children unattended.

The way in which child and adult disarmament were disaggregated also disadvantaged some girls and women. This division was informed by the international legal distinction between child and adult rather than Sierra Leonean understandings of these categories. Joseph Momoh, founder of Children Associated with the War, illustrated the gap between local perceptions of "child" and "adult" and Western legal definitions. He explained that for many ethnic groups in Sierra Leone there are cultural ceremonies that mark the passing from childhood to adulthood. For most ethnic groups in the country, ceremonies take place within separate male and female secret societies.

These groups are responsible for educating members about cultural traditions, histories, and skills and trades deemed essential for survival and success within the community. There has been growing scrutiny of women's secret societies because some ceremonies marking a female's transition to adulthood, or *bondo* ceremonies, include female circumcision. *Bondo* ceremonies were disrupted during the civil conflict; as a result, there was some confusion as to the status of women and girls in their communities and their eligibility for the DDR. Momoh explains:

> Some girls that were around the age of sixteen would feel strange going through the DDR because they were not seen as adults because they didn't go through ceremonies but they didn't see themselves as children because they had had sex and some had children. . . . You can have a baby but if you haven't gone through the ceremonies you are not considered mature enough to have a child and you are still considered a child. A mother is someone who has gone through the ceremonies. . . . If you give birth to a child you are not an adult and you cannot carry out adult responsibilities so that is why some parents don't want to send their girls through the DDR because their girls had babies and it was shameful.[51]

At the end of the war twenty-eight of the fifty women I interviewed would have been under the age of eighteen and therefore defined as a child according to the Convention on the Rights of the Child. These women would have been eligible for the children's DDR; however, a surprising number did not see themselves as children either because they were already mothers or, because of the loss of parents, some had taken on adult roles for a number of years.

Even when the failures of the DDR program were acknowledged, there was little effort to alter the program to better attract women and girls or to meet female beneficiaries' needs. When Rev. Hassan Mansaray with CIS was asked if the local and international organizations understood that the DDR was neglecting women and girls, he replied, "People realized it." He went on to explain, "NCDDR was a very big organization. Too big, and when it has focused its attention on one area it is very difficult for you to turn its attention to another area. It had a lifetime for the commission to complete. . . . so it is like an elephant, it is difficult to turn an elephant's attention to you when it has focused on another area."

Women Assess Their "Empowerment"

Personal interviews are rare within research and scholarship on female soldiers and the DDR. Moreover, to my knowledge, there have been no interviews with female soldiers about the notion of empowerment or their perception of DDR in relation to empowerment. Given the excessive use of empowerment in development and that DDR is framed as a source of empowerment for ex-soldiers, it seems valuable to ask both beneficiaries of the program and those who should have been included in the program for their assessment of the empowerment potential of DDR.

Of the seventy-five female combatants interviewed for this book, only a handful went through the DDR. Many of those who did not participate had formed opinions about the program based on their own knowledge of the process or on family members' or friends' experiences. For example, when asked about the DDR, Sadie, who did not go through the process, reported, "I know a lot of them [that went through the DDR], our neighbors. They didn't help them at all—nothing! They are in the streets."

When I asked the women who did participate in the DDR if these programs met their needs, some of their responses included the following: "Not me at all,"[52] "No, it just added salt into injuries,"[53] and "I was grossly disappointed by the way I was treated and the premature and abrupt way the program was ended."[54] These women had much to say about the weaknesses of the reintegration portion of the DDR. Several were convinced that reintegration funds were directed "to families of program officials."[55] Others mentioned corruption, misdirection, and mismanagement of funds as a weakness of the program.[56] One woman described the last phase of the DDR as "witch hunt reintegration" due to the stigmatization that resulted from being associated with it.[57]

Another respondent claimed that combatants were misinformed about the DDR process, and in some cases certain beneficiaries faced discrimination.[58] Fatima, another former combatant who was recruited as an arms bearer for the RUF, admitted that the program was useful; however, she also noted that "the small amount of money I received when I surrendered with my weapon could not keep me going."

One former soldier in particular, Sarah, fought against pro-government forces and took part in looting, burning civilians and public premises, and maiming civilians. Sarah participated in the DDR but concluded that the program was poorly organized and did not distribute resources evenly to former combatants. She reported she was "grossly abused even by program officers" at reintegration facilities. She also noted, "We were treated as public nuisances and ridiculed." Sarah felt the program ended far too quickly to be of use for her, and she considered her current situation to be far worse than before the conflict: "Now I live with war stigma and trauma." Sarah argued that the situation for women in general has not improved: "In our community decision making is not an active ingredient in the life of women . . . they are nothing but property . . . even the affluent struggle to take part in decision making."

Mary participated in the war as a soldier for two years; her activities included fighting and killing. When she went to the demobilization center, she was held for two months and given a small amount of money; however, after the program she could not find her mother and discovered that her father had died during the conflict. Mary noted that she had been counseled "not to do bad" but argued that rather than such advice, she needed assistance to help raise children that she gave birth to as a result of relationships with rebels. She noted that men had the advantage of being able to leave behind their children while women were left to care for them.

When I asked both those who went through the program and those who did not how to improve the disarmament and reintegration process for women, the respondents' suggestions included providing lucrative jobs, education, and psychological support; ensuring information gets to female combatants; and having more local input into the process. Women consistently called for ongoing assistance with finding work as well as the desire for "not just a job, but a good job."[59] Referring to programs that trained women in tailoring and offered to buy them sewing machines, one interviewee explained that homeless women will still "need a place to put these machines."[60]

A common suggestion for improving programs was that education should have been provided for free and for all female soldiers.[61] For example, Catherine, a former soldier who "had an AK-47" and destroyed property and "gained a wealth of military tactics" while with the Sierra Leone Army for one year declared that she felt she was on the right track while in the army and has no remorse. Her desire, in terms of reintegration, was to be given access to formal education.

One woman claimed that a "sense of belonging" is a significant need for reintegrating soldiers; another argued that girls had to be given more priority in future programs.[62] Many women described their current situation as desperate and, in most cases, worse than in the wartime period. For example,

Zainab reported that in Sierra Leone "women are considered not capable to give and have job opportunities as they are just good to be wives cooking and giving birth to children."[63] Another woman described how women in Sierra Leone are "meant to be seen, not heard."[64]

Evaluating Empowerment

The success of reintegration programs in empowering women has been limited, at best, for several reasons. First, these programs offered women inadequate training options that were highly gendered and largely nonlucrative. The lack of market assessment meant that trades were chosen for females based on gendered ideas of what women should do in the marketplace rather than an assessment of trades that would allow them to make money and succeed in the marketplace. The small number of trades also meant that there was an overabundance of women trained in specific areas, thereby diluting the worth of their trade.

Second, the reintegration process for female soldiers was not inclusive or representative. Despite the fact that the planners and initiators of the DDR in Sierra Leone advertised their intentions to include local knowledge and focus on indigenous values and trades, the direction for the reintegration process came almost entirely from above. That is, the main funding partners for the DDR—the World Bank and the UN—dictated what trades would be funded, the duration of the programs, and which soldiers were eligible. The World Bank and the UN—two organizations claiming to be "gender mainstreaming," inclusive, and concerned with "the local"—dictated that women soldiers should be trained as *gara* tie-dyers, seamstresses, caterers, soap makers, and weavers. This meant that even if local organizations wanted to offer alternative options for skills training, they would not be eligible for funding from either of these major organizations. "Local knowledge" about what skills were valued or needed was never really assessed or taken into account during the reintegration process in Sierra Leone. Instead, it was constrained and shaped by the biggest funding parties.

Third, microcredit initiatives, which were designed to empower former female soldiers, were not designed to give women economic independence; rather, they assumed, and required, a nuclear family structure. Microcredit programs, although highly lauded in many development contexts, represented the "return to normal" for women in Sierra Leone in a very specific way. The explicit goal of the microcredit programs was to give women the means to provide financial support for their families in order to reduce family pressures on male ex-combatants.[65] The implicit assumption of this objective is that female soldiers are married, that they wish to stay married, and that their primary objective is to support their husband, who is presumed to be the principal wage earner. This program is a prime example of the disciplinary potential of empowerment programs, which impose conditions on participants based on Western-liberal gendered notions of the nuclear family.

Conclusion

The DDR, which should have been a source of change and opportunity for female soldiers, failed women on a number of fronts. First, it failed to attract and include many female soldiers. Second, even for those female soldiers who did participate, the DDR was a source of social restriction rather than empowerment. It was neither directed by local actors nor responsive to women's input. Instead, by choosing highly gendered training options, the DDR for women carried explicit messages about appropriate gender role, and emphasized social reintegration—all in the name of empowerment.

Development actors in Sierra Leone made little effort to understand the motivations and experiences of women and girls during the conflict. In turn, initiatives designed to address women's and girls' needs and to "empower" them post–armed conflict were ill informed at best. Moreover, there has been little investigation into the possibility that war was empowering for female soldiers—despite evidence that, in some cases, female soldiers had more access to resources, more social freedom, and more political power during the official war than during the so-called pre- and postwar context. Empowerment can neither be identified as a legitimate objective nor praised as a sign of progress within development approaches in the absence of dialogue between development actors and the beneficiaries of empowerment programs.

Empowerment initiatives for female soldiers did not respond to obvious needs; rather, they encouraged and regulated women to participate in and comply with established social and economic relationships. In addition, empowerment discourses serve to discipline subjects according to specific neoliberal notions of progress and social order. As a result, rather than offering the potential for change, inclusion, and representation, programs designed to empower female soldiers conveyed explicit messages about the social and familial relationships that are "normal" at the same time as they off-loaded responsibility for development from development actors to the individual. In this way, the boom in empowerment projects for female soldiers has been a bust in terms of offering real possibilities for change and representation.

5

Securitization and Desecuritization

Female Soldiers and the Reconstruction of Women

We didn't have many girls [at the reintegration center]. I don't know what happened to the ex-combatant girls and ladies. Amongst the group that was brought to us, the [number of] girls [was] not even ten. Some of the most vicious soldiers and commanders were women. I'm still wondering what happened to the ex-combatant ladies and girls because the number that showed up [was] too small, which means that we have lots and lots of these women and girls that are not reintegrated.[1]

Saphie was conscripted by the AFRC/RUF at the age of fourteen. Her roles during the conflict included fighting, gun trafficking, acting as a "bush wife," and acting as a spy. Saphie explained why she did not go through the DDR in the following way: "I was excluded by my commander as they took my gun from me—the symbol to guarantee me to be part of the reintegration program." She heard that the program was useful and was especially envious of the $300 disarmament payment.[2] *Saphie also heard that ex-combatants were reunited with their parents and were given medical attention and clothing. For Saphie, the strengths of the program included the huge amount of international support; however, she felt that the program did not fulfill its promises to ex-combatants. She felt that female soldiers were deceived and were not given sufficient information about the program. She asserted that "girl soldiers were part of the 'real' people that mattered to the program." She also felt that most reintegration initiatives ended prematurely and heard about embezzlement of program funds by officials. Saphie reported that she finds her current situation frustrating as she is "just trying to survive" despite poverty.*

Lene Hansen proposes that "a critical discourse might start by challenging the key representations of identity that underpin the policy in question."[3] This chapter investigates the gendered assumptions that underpin policy makers' responses to the question "Why did so few women and girls participate in the

>> 85

DDR in Sierra Leone?" Through a critical discourse analysis of news reports and NGO, INGO, government, and aid agency documents and policies, as well as existing literature on the disarmament process in Sierra Leone, I show how the majority of the policy responses to this question send three specific gendered messages: first, they perpetuate the notion of women as ideal victims lacking agency during war; second, these accounts of the DDR presume that the program was effective and that the problem was that women and girls were not sufficiently included in the process; third, those organizations that acknowledged the need to address women's and girls' specific gendered needs never asked women or girls what these needs were, implying that gender sensitivity can be achieved without speaking to beneficiaries.

In this chapter I compare these explanations with female soldiers' own rationalizations of why they did not participate in the DDR. The diverse, complex, rational, and emotional responses to this question stand in stark contrast to the sterilized and oversimplified reports of women and girls being "left behind" or "forgotten" by the DDR. In addition, these answers show the inadequacy of current lists of "lessons learned" that local and international organizations offered with regard to female soldiers and post-conflict policy making. In turn, these stories and responses confirm the importance of speaking to women and girls rather than speaking for them.

Engendering the DDR: Why Women Were Overlooked

As illustrated in chapter 4, the DDR in Sierra Leone was advertised as a source of empowerment for both men and women. The DDR in this country was also largely described as a success and has been recommended as a model for future programs.[4] Despite its praises, one of the lessons learned from the DDR has been drawn from its treatment of women and girls. As already noted, the exact number of women and girls involved in the fighting forces is unknown; however, estimates range from 10 percent up to 50 percent in various armed factions.[5] These numbers are not reflected in DDR statistics. Of the approximately 75,000 adult combatants disarmed, just under 5,000 were females.[6] The number of girls that went through the children's DDR was abysmal; of the 6,845 child soldiers disarmed, only 8 percent were girls. UNICEF has admitted, "DDR programmes have consistently failed to attract female combatants . . . . Sierra Leone was no exception."[7]

Along with a growing body of research that critically examines gender and the DDR in Sierra Leone, one of the most common explanations for the low numbers of females in the DDR is the argument that women and girls were not "real" soldiers. As mentioned in chapter 3, women and girls soldiers were often classified as camp followers, abductees, unaccompanied children, women associated with the fighting forces, or sex slaves. As a result, the low numbers of girls and women who participated in the DDR are seen as an accurate reflection of the numbers of females who were "actually" soldiers—the presumption being that other women who were with the rebels acted in support roles or were generally victims coerced into a male-dominated war.

Another justification given to explain the low numbers of women in the DDR was that women and girls were simply overlooked. In particular, women and girls who did not go through the DDR have been portrayed as victims left behind and neglected by the local and international community. For example, the UNICEF report on the lessons learned from the DDR cites the consideration of gender and the inclusion of girls as a major shortcoming of the programming. In fact, one of the major programs initiated in response to criticisms about the inclusion of girls and women in the DDR was called Girls Left Behind. According to UNICEF, this program was created to target "young girls and women who were either still living with their captors or who had been abducted (before the age of 18) and had been released or escaped."[8] The program was designed to be a short-term, intensive intervention "for abducted girls and young women to ensure their protection and reintegration and to offer them basic education and skills training."[9] Eligibility for this program required victimhood. Many women and girls were abducted during the war, but some also joined willingly. Furthermore, women and girls were victimized during the war, but, as my interviews show, many also gained a significant amount of power and authority as a result of their combat roles. Creating a program for abducted girls "left behind" is exclusive and perpetuates gender stereotypes about women and girls as the "ideal" victims in war.

Assuming women and girl soldiers were "left behind" also denies any agency on the part of females during the war and implies that the DDR problem with women and girls was one of inclusion, not program design or gender awareness. There is an assumption that women and girls were either victims caught up in the fray of a male-dominated conflict or were left behind by programs that likely would have benefited them in the same way they benefited male soldiers. These explanations ignore how socially constructed ideas about the roles and place of women and men during war impact policies, depictions, and our ability to accept and acknowledge violent female soldiers with agency. My interviews with local officials who worked with female soldiers and with female soldiers themselves disrupt these stereotypes of women and girls as exclusively passive victims of the conflict.

Women Give Their Own Reasons and Tell Their Own Stories of Disarmament

My interviews with female soldiers in Sierra Leone demonstrate not only that women were actively involved in combat but also that the answer to the question "Why did so few women and girls go through the DDR?" requires a more in-depth answer than "They were left behind." This chapter will look at some of the common themes within these answers, including confusion regarding eligibility criteria, fear of stigma, misinformation, and pride. Most women gave a variety of seemingly practical or understandable reasons for not participating in the program. No women I spoke with indicated they felt "left out" of the DDR, and very few indicated they thought the DDR would have been helpful for them.

One of the more common reasons women listed for not participating in the DDR was that they did not possess a gun at the time of demobilization. During the first two phases of the DDR, one of the requirements for entry into the process was the possession of a gun. For children, the possession of a gun was never a requirement; however, many children were not clear on this fact. DDR procedures for children defined eligibility as follows: "aged 7 or above; have learned to 'cock and load'; have been trained; have spent 6 months or above in the fighting forces."[10] Organizers of the DDR soon recognized several factors that made the requirement of a weapon dysfunctional: first, not all soldiers used or possessed guns; second, a variety of rudimentary weapons such as machetes were commonly used by rebels; third, many soldiers who wanted to participate in the DDR had escaped or left their armed group and were unlikely to hold weapons. Given that the conflict in Sierra Leone lasted more than eleven years, involved various armed factions, and erupted in several phases, each individual combatant did not necessarily possess his or her own weapon.

As a result, during the last phase of the DDR, ex-combatants were not required to hand in a weapon. Despite the change in official policy, the primary understanding of the DDR for a striking number of the women interviewed was that it was "just about men with guns"[11] or that it was a "gun for money"[12] program directed at male rebels. For example, Kadie participated as a child soldier for the RUF for five months. Her mother and husband were both killed during the war. She thought one of the weaknesses of the DDR program was that one needed to have a gun to participate. She did not know any women who participated in the DDR and said that another reason women could not participate was that they did not want to leave their children. She felt that the DDR could have been improved. Kadie criticized the program for providing disparate resources and attention to men and women, adding, "They disarm the boys but the ladies remain."

Although numerous women I interviewed admitted to carrying and using guns, several admitted they had their guns taken away from them before the DDR, and others told me they left their weapons behind when they escaped from their armed group. In some of these cases, commanders or comrades deliberately took weapons from women and girls before the disarmament process so they would not be eligible for the program. In addition, both males and females who performed support roles during the conflict (including domestic tasks, acting as spies or messengers and looters) may or may not have ever possessed a gun. Sasha was one of the women who explained that she did not participate in the DDR because she did not have a weapon. She was conscripted by the AFRC/RUF at the age of fourteen, and her roles during the conflict included fighting, gun trafficking, "acting as a bush wife," and spying. Despite her role as a fighter, she reported that her commander deliberately prevented her from participating in the DDR: "I was excluded by my commander as they [sic] took my gun from me—the symbol to guarantee me to be part of the reintegration program." For her, the strengths of the program included the huge amount of international support; however, she believed that the program did not fulfill its promises to ex-combatants. She felt that female soldiers were deceived and were not given sufficient information about the program, claiming that "girl soldiers were not part of the 'real' people that mattered to the program." She also felt that most reintegration initiatives ended prematurely and had heard about embezzlement of program funds by officials. She reported that she finds her current situation frustrating as she is "just trying to survive" despite poverty.[13]

Many women and girls had escaped or left their armed group before the DDR was established and mentioned this as the reason for not participating in the DDR. Of the fifty women I interviewed in Makeni, forty-four had escaped from their respective armed groups. Women who had escaped from their armed group avoided the DDR not only because they did not have a weapon but also because they had returned to their families and had begun to disassociate themselves from the armed groups. For example, Salamatu explained that she did not see herself as eligible for the disarmament process because she had escaped and "wasn't with the rebels any longer."[14] Salamatu was part of a large group of students who had been captured. She was approximately sixteen years old at the time of her abduction. She did domestic work for a rebel group under the command of "Superman," the head rebel in the area. Near the end of the conflict she escaped and found her parents. She explained, "When I saw my parents I didn't want to go [to the DDR], I just wanted to return to them."

In a way, escapee women left the DDR behind because they no longer saw themselves as soldiers or no longer wanted to be connected with armed forces. It makes sense that women—some of whom had risked their lives to escape —would not want to rejoin an armed group for a disarmament process. In order for the DDR to have met the needs of the large number of women and girls who escaped from the armed forces, the DDR should have specifically targeted escapees by making efforts to inform them that they were still eligible for the DDR and that their safety would be ensured during the process.

Women also mentioned that their fear of stigmatization kept them away from disarmament facilities. There were sensitization campaigns encouraging Sierra Leoneans to accept former soldiers back into their communities in order to help the nation move forward. Sulay Sesay, an organizer with the DDR, explained: "We came up with many sensitization sessions on forgiveness—much of the information got out through discussions on the radio. We also worked with Talking Drum Studio."[15] Despite these efforts, former soldiers—particularly women—faced stigma through their association with armed groups. Sesay admitted that former soldiers still faced isolation and stigmatization post-conflict:

> It was not easy for us to take ex-combatants back. Some community members would tell us "don't bring him/her here." We had a lady who was a former RUF leader—her children were in the child welfare center in Makeni. Now she wanted to take her children and herself back to her community. So we did some advance sensitization, and each time the chief would say "don't bring her here," "we don't want her here." We eventually convinced him to accept her.

Alimatu, who was abducted at the age of sixteen, was with the RUF for three years. She stated that it was possible for her to participate in the DDR and that she was more concerned with finding her parents at the end of the war. She knew some friends who went through the DDR and said they were encouraged to forget what happened during the civil conflict. Alimatu also knew many other women who did not go through the DDR and said that most of them are "doing nothing." She went to find her parents after the war, and initially they resisted her return; she described having to beg her parents to accept her. Alimatu criticized the DDR for continuing to focus on men and "forgetting" women and their participation in the conflict.

Some of the interviewees described the DDR as "shameful" and spoke about the negative effect it would have on their families. For example, Tryphena described the potential impact of participating in the DDR: "[The community] will know that you are a rebel and you will feel uneasy in the community—you will be faced with fear." Also, some women were anxious to start a new life and to break ties with their lives as soldiers. Their association with programs designed for former soldiers meant they were continually identified with the conflict. This was not an option for women who "didn't want people to know that [they] took part in [the] mad war."[16] One woman told me she did not want to be "seen publicly as an ex-combatant" out of "fear of retaliation"[17] from community members or other rebel factions. Similarly, a young woman told me she had reason to believe that if she showed up at the DDR she would be killed by the Special Security Death Squad, a brutal, specialized armed group. Given the fact that the DDR took place at the dubious end of a ten-year civil war, some women and girls were not convinced that the fighting was truly over and did not want to label themselves openly at the DDR out of concern for their security.

Isatu was a female soldier who escaped from the rebel forces. She was abducted at the age of ten and cooked and did other domestic work for the rebels. She explained, "During the disarmament the rebels handed me over to some white lady, but I can't remember her name....Maybe the white person worked with the DDR." She ran away from this woman and the rebel group. She was pleased with the DDR because it gave her an opportunity to escape. Isatu added, "Since the rebels were paid, that is good because it was incentive for them not to commit crimes again. But many men sold their start-up packages after the war, and that is the bad of the program." She explained that she was happy to escape and did not want to participate in the DDR because it would mean "showing [her] face where the rebels were at the DDR.... I did not want that stigma to be with me that I went through the DDR."

In terms of the structure of the program, one of the procedures that was linked to stigmatization was the identification process for former soldiers. During the disarmament, each soldier had his or her picture taken and was given an ID card, which made the soldier eligible for training programs, financial assistance, or start-up packages. Sulay Sesay admitted that the ID cards could be used to detect former soldiers and became a source of shame for some individuals. He clarified, "At some points the identity cards were bad because if [soldiers] are traveling up-country and people see the identity cards they will stop them and identify them as former soldiers. So many soldiers prepared to stay in Freetown."

Several of the women I talked to expressed unease with the identification process. Hawa believed that "many" women did not go through the DDR because they were ashamed of the photo ID card they would be issued. She said former soldiers were worried this card would continue to distinguish them as soldiers. Aminata reiterated this point: "When I heard about the DDR, I wasn't agreeing to go through the DDR. We were ashamed of having our faces to be on the computer because they take a photo of each person that went through the DDR. I felt nervous that our photos would be kept by immigration and that we would never be able to leave the country.[18]

In addition to stigmatization, escaping, and not possessing a gun, women had several unexpected reasons for not participating in the DDR. To begin with, a significant number of the women I interviewed had an extraordinarily negative perception of the DDR and did not see it as an attractive option for them post-conflict. For example, descriptions of the program included "a trap to screen antigovernment combatants"[19] and a program that "paid rebels" for burning houses and killing families. Some women claimed they were not convinced the program benefited anybody other than international NGOs. For example, Sonia[20] reported, "We were used as everything for them [NGOs/international aid community] to have and be everything they want to be in their war and political ambitions." [21]The program was also described as a tactical "use of ex-combatants as tools for fund-raising" for NGO workers to "enrich themselves."[22] Another woman commented, "All I saw was expensive vehicles being used by those NGOs and so much bureaucracy."[23]

One prominent concern expressed by former female soldiers was their distrust of the promises made by the Sierra Leone government and the organizations involved in the DDR. Some witnessed the first phases of the DDR while they were still involved with the fighting forces and concluded that the "flamboyant promises"[24] made to ex-combatants were not fulfilled. This distrust also stemmed from accusations of corruption and beliefs that "funds [were] directed to families of program officials."[25] These testimonies demonstrate that negative perceptions impacted women's and girls' decisions not to participate in the DDR. In these cases, these women did not feel left out of the process; rather, they chose to avoid it because they were critical of the program and the way it was implemented.

While those who were critical chose to avoid the program, other women were prevented from participating in the DDR by their parents, their husbands, or their commanders. Francis Lahai was confident that many women had been thwarted from the DDR by other members of their armed group:

> One thing I noted about the DDR program, even though it had done so much work ... the number of children it addressed really was very small—particularly the girls. Most of the girls were not disarmed because when they were abducted they were taken to the bush [where] they became combatants as well as sex slaves to the commanders, and during the disarmament and the DDR program these girls were prevented from going to disarm because they were already wives of the commanders.

Edward Anague from CEDA confirmed that some women and girls were prevented from participating by their families or husbands: "The families threatened [former soldiers] and said that if we went through they would be harmed or arrested."

Mamsu was another female soldier who was discouraged from participating in the DDR by her family. She gave the following account: "I was deterred to reintegration facilities because my parents thought I will later be targeted." Mamsu identified as a soldier "because I was an ammunition and arms carrier and was a conscript to do spying." When asked about her roles during the war, she listed the following activities: "I was a spy and murdered children, I was a combatant, I was a bush wife to many male fighters." Mamsu reflected that the DDR "would have been useful if what was proposed for the reintegration process was implemented to the letter practically without exclusion or bias...[and] if the packages of reintegration were directly given to us women soldiers." She complained that "very few girls were given consideration to go through the reintegration process even though we were the tools of the war used by both pro-government and anti-government forces." Mamsu also felt that female soldiers were treated differently than males because "the boy soldiers were considered rude and more dangerous to security."

Esther provided the following account of her life during the war: "I took part in the mad war in Sierra Leone when I was recruited for a special body unit by the Kamajors." She listed her combatant activities as spying, toting looted property, being "used as target for ambush," and being used as a cook and sex slave for commanders. When asked why she did not participate in the DDR, Esther replied, "The Kamajors prevented me because they have a taboo that they do not touch or come close to women but it was a lie to fake self-praise." Esther admitted she did not know the details of the DDR, but she had heard of the foreign involvement and the large amounts of money directed through the program. She expressed frustration at how females were treated in post–armed conflict Sierra Leone: "All of us were combatants but treated as housewives and sex slaves."

Pride was an additional theme in the responses to questions about the DDR. Several women I interviewed indicated either that they had "better plans" for themselves than the DDR or that they felt the DDR was somehow "below them." For example, one woman told me she avoided the DDR because she had been promised by the head of the Civil Defence Forces that she would be given "a lucrative house and educational support"[26] if she remained with the forces. Theresa told me she had money from the war and did not need the handouts offered at the DDR. A few women had made plans to go on missions in the Ivory Coast and Guinea or had hoped to travel to South Africa with the Executive Outcome Forces—an armed group from South Africa. These women were not left out of the DDR but had charted courses they saw as more attractive than participating in the process.

Some women even reported that they felt they were "above" or "beyond" the DDR due to their status or the power they held. One woman explained to me that she thought her "looks would carry [her] a long way"[27] and that she did not need the resources offered by the DDR. Another informed me that she was "too popular"[28] to go to the DDR and that people would recognize her and target her and her family. After reading numerous accounts of the oppression and victimization of women during and after the conflict, I was not expecting to hear the pride women associate with their role as a soldier. For some women who had achieved higher ranks within the warring factions, the notion of attending the DDR with lower-ranking soldiers was insulting. One woman explained, "I was not convinced to see myself parade before people I had authority over for years."[29] Several other women mentioned their disapproval of the "segregation within the command ranks" at the DDR.[30] The lessons learned from the DDR in Sierra Leone do not account for these shifts in power that occurred during the civil war (and numerous other wars) and the difficulty women had with losing this power.

It is possible to catalogue the previous categories of answers for why women did not participate in the DDR; however, it should be noted that the answers the majority of women gave to this question were complex and included more than one reason. Glenis Taylor of UNICEF gave an account of the complexity and diversity of reasons for why women may have avoided or chosen not to participate in the DDR:

> We had an interim care center for girl mothers before peace was declared. A lot of them were ex-combatants who didn't go through the DDR and so the reasons they gave were stigma and another was fear of being a burden on their family. They said they have never been to school, and they don't have any skills and "now I am going back with an extra mouth to feed. I know times were tough before and now I'm going back with an extra mouth and I don't want to take my parents through that." Another thing, for some of the girls there were cases of girls leaving the center and returning to the bush. They said "oh in the bush we can get three meals a day—when you come home it is just one meal a day." Some were the wives of commanders and had a certain status and could give orders and so some of them found it difficult to fit in. I know about one or two found it difficult to settle down after—they were used to being showered with gifts and privileges so for some of them they are used to quick money and so they found it difficult to focus and settle down to learn a skill.

Abu J. Conte, a program manager for a child protection program in Makeni, Sierra Leone, also contended that there were various reasons for the low number of women and girls who participated in the DDR. He specified that "some [women and girls] were taken from families and schools. [Some] came back with babies, some felt they were a part of the business of war. Some melted into the communities, some were afraid to go back to families, some stayed with captors, some stayed alone."

Although there were some common themes to the answers, many women offered multifaceted answers to the question "Why did you not participate in the DDR?" For example, Mabintu, a former member of the RUF who once poisoned captured war prisoners, told me she did not participate in the DDR for several reasons: "I had no gun to qualify me to disarm.... I was not used to public gatherings.... Not to bring negative stigma to my family." Similarly, Marion was recruited by Ulimo Johnson in Kailahun as a special "body" unit used to plan and carry out attacks on public places. She described the DDR program as "not clear" and added that she did not participate because her commander told her to refuse and that her commander had a mission in the Ivory Coast. Similarly, Isha joined the AFRC in her early teens. She reported that she burned public and private premises as well as living pro-government forces. Isha refused to go through the DDR, claiming,

"I cannot trust the program." Isha also mentioned her fear of the stigma that would be cast on her and her family if she publicly participated in the DDR. For her, the DDR was merely "information propaganda and money-making." She claimed that "boys had more support" because they were feared while females were not. Jamalitu offered an even more complex story. She reported that she was recruited by the CDF to "do concoctions in the holy shrine." She listed the following reasons for not attending the DDR: "I was warned not to appear; rather the devil will consume me.... I feared the demon of protection during the war will consume me and my family and all CDF."

Isatu, a former rebel, also told me her family was "not happy to see their daughter in that [DDR] camp." She added, "Even when the rebels captured me, the family was not happy about that, so when my family saw me they took the weapon from me, asked me to give the weapon back to the husband that gave it to me, and I didn't go to the disarmament." Isatu also shared that she knew of a fire at a DDR center that had been started by rebels: "The rebels started the fire while people were learning." It destroyed the whole center and made her feel nervous that it was dangerous to attend the DDR. "I heard that there were many sewing machines being sent to a program so it should have been so helpful, but I heard about the fire and then was afraid because the rebels were misbehaving."

These interviews indicate the complexities associated with women's decisions not to go to the DDR. Programs for female victims of the war, abducted girls and women, and girls left behind were developed in the absence of women's own accounts of what roles they took up during the war, how they perceived the DDR, and why they did not participate in the DDR. Although women's choices to participate or not were made in extremely constrained circumstances, by ignoring women's accounts of why they made these decisions, useful lessons to be derived from the DDR become buried. The decisions that female soldiers made in relation to the DDR should be seen as political decisions and must be taken into account when considering the effectiveness and impact of the DDR.

Conclusion

Sierra Leone's disarmament process should not be hailed as a success or exported as a model for other countries without accounting for women's and girls' own depictions of their roles and experiences during the conflict. The negative impacts of the DDR in Sierra Leone on women suggest that there is a need to reconsider the positive association of reintegration and reconstruction with progress and development.

Attention to women's and girls' experiences would produce a more complicated understanding of women (who can be both victims and aggressors/agents) and of conflict (as consuming the entire society and extending beyond the official time lines of war). Complicating our understanding of females and the conflicts they participate in would inspire different kinds of questions and policies post–armed conflict. For example, this analysis demonstrates that it is crucial to disarm, demobilize, and reintegrate female former combatants on the terms of their needs and their experiences in the conflict if the society is to transition from conflict to peace. Another important realization is that the needs of former female combatants cannot be determined solely by understanding the ways in which they have been victimized; it is also important to consider the ways in which they have participated in the conflict.

6

Securitizing Sex?

Rethinking Wartime Sexual Violence

"We have girls that had their breast tattooed with RUF. During the war, if you have on your skin anything that entails RUF you will definitely be killed or sent to jail and so it is one of the means that the rebels used for these sex slaves to write on their physical skin RUF because of that the girls will not have any way to escape after they have been kidnapped. We faced so many problems with their behavior and so what we did was include in their curriculum some religious and moral skills because some of them were very hostile and some of them find it very difficult to remarry knowing that they already have children that do not have fathers. Especially for those that have writings on their bodies it is difficult. One of the girls took a hot charcoal mass and placed it on her breast to burn out the writing but it didn't go."[1]

Fatima was a child soldier for the RUF for two years, beginning when she was fourteen. She held a combat role with the rebel forces and admitted to destroying property and abusing drugs. She summarized the process by which she came to be a soldier and her experience with the RUF as follows: "I was abducted and later forced to join their group. I was persistently raped. I was trained to use a weapon. I was forced to go on long-distance treks on foot." She told reintegration authorities that she was interested in some sort of formal education and being reunited with a parent.

The question "Why is rape deemed an effective tool of war?" has not been sufficiently explored and has been limited by traditional conflict and security metaphors. Continuing to focus on Sierra Leone, this chapter will explore dominant approaches to wartime rape and offer a new framework from which to consider why rape is used as a tool of war and why it has been a part of militant strategies through history. Questioning the utility of wartime rape and the possible strategic gains to be had from its use poses various difficult and sensitive challenges; however, examining the strategic use of wartime rape points to embedded patriarchal norms that are laid bare during conflict. This approach also highlights the linkages between sex, the family, and international politics and shows that relationships and norms typically classified as private, domestic matters—such as those associated with conjugal order—are central to understanding warfare politics and strategy.

The starting point of this analysis is the argument that, like other tools of war, rape is used to create disorder. In turn, it is useful to examine the forms of sexual regulation that make up the "order" at which rape is directed. First, this understanding gives a new perspective to the strategic function of rape. Second, it could be helpful for those attempting to construct effective mechanisms to both limit and reprimand the use of wartime rape. Focusing on the use of rape during the civil conflict in Sierra Leone, I argue here that rape was an effective tool of war primarily because it violated norms associated with conjugal order, including legal and normative legacies associated with marriage and the family left from British colonizers.

Jacqueline Stevens argues that the institution of marriage guarantees men access to women's bodies and labor.[2] Pointing to historic and current marriage and paternity laws, Stevens reminds us that rape within marriage was (and in many countries still is) seen as an impossibility because sex is seen to be granted to men within the institution of marriage. As indicated in chapter 1, Stevens argues that marriage—by definition—creates unequal gender relationships and roles guaranteeing men access to women's labor and bodies.[3] Building on this point, I argue that part of conjugal order—or the variable norms associated with marriage, paternity, and the family—involves bestowing men, through the institution of marriage, with a significant amount of power over, and access to, the labor of women. As a result, the act of rape becomes an effective strategy because it creates *dis*order by desecrating the authority and property assured to males, as well as violating established norms relating to the family. In turn, the act of creating insecurity or disorder is intimately implicated in, and in fact dependent on, what is typically considered domestic politics. The very relationships that are established through marriage and paternity laws—which are presented as prepolitical and private—provide the motivation, justification, and tactical advantage for one of the oldest and most consistent strategies of war—rape.

Furthermore, wartime rape is an effective strategy for perpetrators because the act has long-term and extensive impacts. In fact, security and development studies largely ignore the broader security impacts of sexual violence within war-affected communities. This includes stigmatization and marginalization not only for the victim of the rape but also for her family, including any children to whom she may give birth. The "collateral damages" that stem from rape are all too often conceptualized as social matters rather than as sources of significant insecurity. Exploring gender orders and the widespread impacts of rape also helps demonstrate that there is continuity not only between sexual violence within and outside of war but also between the regulation of sex and the family within and outside of war.

In addition to questions of the utility of wartime rape, this chapter explores the implications of ignoring gender hierarchies and failing to see the interconnectedness of the so-called domestic realm, including sex and marriage, to warfare politics and security. Expired notions of the private and public realms in international politics have largely limited traditional and even critical approaches to wartime rape within international relations and security studies. In turn, this chapter utilizes the concept of conjugal order to better understand the relationship between sex, rape, and international politics.

This chapter begins with an overview of dominant explanations of wartime rape. Following this, Sierra Leone is presented as a case study that exemplifies the hypothesis that marriage and family law are directly related to the strategic use of wartime rape. This analysis takes an intertextual approach, which weaves together research from program documents and policies related to wartime rape, existing literature on wartime rape, and unstructured interviews with NGO workers, aid staff, and government officials conducted in Sierra Leone in 2005.

Research on Wartime Rape

Since Susan Brownmiller's[4] seminal book on rape, *Against Our Will: Men, Women and Rape*, was published, there has been a proliferation of scholarship in this area. This expanding body of scholarship includes perspectives on wartime rape in relation to international law,[5] human rights,[6] nationalism and identity,[7] and violence against women more broadly.[8] Although an exhaustive discussion of these contributions is not possible here, identifying major themes illustrates the need to consider the relationship of marriage and the family to wartime rape. One dominant theme within scholarship on wartime sexual violence is a focus on patriarchy. Feminists like Brownmiller have argued that wartime rape is an expression of institutionalized power hierarchies as well as a signifier of embedded social norms related to masculinity and femininity and women's bodies. This type of research also points to accounts of rapes that portray the act as a demonstration of the perpetrator's masculinity, while the victim and her family—particularly her husband or male relatives—are perceived as feminized.[9]

There are several related discourses at play in this approach to wartime rape. Cynthia Enloe makes a similar argument using very different terminology. Enloe focuses on militarism and militarization as the root of sexualized violence. Militarism refers to the impact of the military and its values on wider social attitudes, behaviors, and practices. A militarized society is one in which behaviors, values, and practices deemed acceptable during conflict become embedded and institutionalized. Enloe argues that militarization results in the legitimization of the use of violence both within and outside of war.[10] According to this approach, a feature of militarized societies is higher instances of domestic violence and rape.[11] In turn, wartime rape can be seen as a "surge" of sexual violence that is standard during peacetime.

Rape is also framed as an extension of war onto the bodies of women. This approach uses language typically associated with traditional warfare, including "borders," "territory," "dominance," "protection," "supremacy," "conquest," and "power," to describe wartime rape. For example, Jan Jindy Pettman argued that wartime rape is an expression of power and supremacy whereby bodies become part of the violent competition for territory and power.[12] Claudia Card makes a similar case that war rape is a symbol of conquest and domination because it indicates an inability of men to protect "their" women.[13] Such discussions of protectionism and the responsibility of men to protect their "property" are pointed to as symbolic of the significance of patriarchal relations in war.[14]

Those who describe wartime rape as a tool of war represent another approach to this issue.[15] There have been historical accounts of the use of wartime rape as a strategy and tool of war. For example, in the sixteenth century, commentator Francisco de Victoria posited that committing rape could evoke courage in troops and thereby aid in a successful battle.[16] Recent high levels of sexual violence in ethnic conflict, including in Rwanda and Bosnia, have inspired scholarship on wartime rape as a tool of genocide and ethnic cleansing, as well as an attack on honor, identity and national or group cohesion.[17] For example, focusing on ethnic conflict, Nancy Farwell depicts war rape as a strategy for "infiltrating or destroying [ethnic] boundaries and attacking the honor of the community and the purity of its lineage."[18] Accounts of wartime rape as a tool of war often center on the impact of the rape instead of describing rape as a side effect of a patriarchal society.[19]

Each of these approaches has something to add to the study of wartime rape generally; however, attributing wartime rape to patriarchy, describing it as a tool of war, or even an extension of war leaves several difficult questions unanswered, including: Are there specific by-products or elements of patriarchy that give meaning to wartime rape? Are there specific customs and institutionalized behaviors that support the notion of women as property or the logic that men are the bearers of national and ethnic identity? I argue that the laws and norms associated with marriage and the family can answer each of these questions about wartime rape.

The Relationship of Marriage and the Family to Rape

There is evidence that rather than just generalized violence against women or visions of "conquest," rape has been used to violate or pervert marriages and traditional family structures throughout history. For example, when Japanese troops committed mass rapes in China in 1937, it was reported that "the Japanese drew sadistic pleasure in forcing men to commit incest—fathers to rape their own daughters, brothers their sisters, sons their mothers."[20] In the Democratic Republic of Congo, similar insights are emerging from recent data on wartime rape during the conflict. A doctor in the region found that rather than motivated by desire, "[rape] is done to destroy completely the social, family fabric of society."[21] In these cases, rape is used to disrupt conjugal order, including the notion of sex within marriage as consensual and sacred, and beliefs associated with heterosexual sex and the nuclear family. This connection will be expanded and supported later through the case study of Sierra Leone.

Further evidence of the link between wartime rape and the family unit can be found by studying international policies and the international laws related to wartime rape. For example, UNICEF explicitly links the family to wartime rape:

> Sexual violation of women erodes the fabric of a community in a way that few weapons can. Rape's damage can be devastating because of the strong communal reaction to the violation and pain stamped on entire families. The harm inflicted in such cases on a woman by a rapist is an attack on her family and culture, as in many societies, women are viewed as repositories of a community's cultural and spiritual values.[22]

Early international legal responses to rape also centered on the family. In 1907 the Hague Convention IV framed wartime rape as an assault on the "honour and rights" of the family rather than a violation of individual rights.[23] Similarly, historically the International Military Tribunal for the Far East (IMTFE) did not consider isolated rape cases; instead, rape was only prosecuted in conjunction with other crimes by classifying it as "inhumane treatment," "ill-treatment," and "failure to respect *family* honor and rights."[24]

Each of these references to the family implies that sex is a part of the natural family unit and that rape is an assault on the entire unit. These descriptions and legal mechanisms are part of the discursive body Stevens attributes to the construction of the family as natural and prepolitical. As she has argued, depicting the family as a "natural" unit assumes that the family is necessary, unchanging, and beyond the realm of political intervention. Subsuming sex within the family unit informs and justifies previous legal frameworks that identified rape as an assault on the family rather than a political act and a violation of individual rights. Furthermore, collapsing sex and the family together into the private and domestic spheres distances them from both the political sphere and what might be considered security priorities.

Sex and the Family in Sierra Leone

In order to explore fully this approach to wartime rape, it is necessary to provide a review of the legacies of colonial law as well as local norms associated with marriage and the family in Sierra Leone. According to Stevens, "The familial nation is not obscure, metaphysical, or difficult to locate. The familial nation exists through practices and often legal documents that set out the kinship rules for political societies."[25] Sierra Leone is no exception to this observation. As mentioned in the introduction to this book, conjugal order is shaped by laws and norms associated with sex and the family. This means that there are multiple iterations of conjugal order reflecting specific cultural and legal contexts. Sierra Leone has four major tribal groups, along with a number of smaller ethnic groups—each with their own distinct practices, norms, and rules. This diversity should result in multiple understandings of conjugal order; however, I argue that conjugal order in Sierra Leone is largely shaped by former colonial laws as well as the current policies of international donors.

As mentioned in chapter 2, during colonization, the British declared the area of Freetown as "the colony," and the rest of the country was classified as "the provinces." Only the colony was subject to British laws, while the peoples of the provinces could govern themselves according to traditional laws and customs. This has produced a unique legal framework in the sense that customary law throughout history has governed the majority of Sierra Leoneans; however, the authority of British law within the capital has had differing impacts on, and relationships with, those customary laws. Most of Freetown's current official legal system is reminiscent of British influence during colonization.

There are three types of marriage in Sierra Leone. "Cultural marriages" involve traditional practices such as the breaking of a kola knot;[26] religious marriages may take place at Christian churches or mosques; and "registry marriages" are ones that are legally registered with the government ministry in Freetown. Although all marriages are binding and recognized, registry marriages are distinct for two main reasons. First, registered marriages are the only type of marriage certified by a government institution. Second, registry marriages are the only type that legally assures a woman access to her husband's property upon his death.

Sexual assault within marriage is still not widely viewed as a criminal offense in Sierra Leone. While women can charge their husbands with abuse under the Offences Against the Persons Act of 1861, it is estimated that less than half of cases are reported and less than a third of reported cases ever reach the courts—particularly in cases of sexual violence.[27] In some areas in Sierra Leone domestic abuse is viewed as "the overt show of a man's love for his wife."[28] When asked about sexual violence within the country, Hamidu Jalloh, country officer for UNDP in Sierra Leone, insisted that before the conflict sexual violence was rare and that the high rates of sexual violence during the conflict and its continued prevalence marked a great departure from typical relations between men and women. He recalled how sexual violence was treated by his community when he was a youth:

> It was a serious offense to rape—the family would take it serious. [Women and girls] were a potential income for the family when marriage occurred. I grew up in a home where the girl was first. Over a period of neglect these structures broke down. If a man raped there was such a heavy price that he would disappear.

Customary law is much more explicitly patriarchal than is civil law. Under customary law, a woman must always be under the protection of a male—typically either her father or her husband.[29] Customary marriage also prevents women from obtaining rights over marital property. According to customary law, marital property, including children, belongs to the husband and his family. Women who cohabitate with a man but never undergo any recognized form of marriage also have no inheritance rights. If there are children from this union, they also may not benefit from their father's estate.[30]

Sierra Leone has four major tribes: Kriole, Shabu, Timne, and Mende. Of these, only the Shabu tribe is matrilineal. For the other three, male children are prioritized, and the oldest son inherits the family's wealth and property. Also, if a woman's husband dies, it is typically her husband's brother who will inherit the husband's wealth and property—unless the husband and wife have a male child who is considered an adult. Customary law solidifies sexual relations within marriage as the only legitimate and authorized type of sexual activity. Further, under customary law it is always an offense for a man to have sex with a woman to whom he is not married, regardless of the age of the woman or her consent.[31]

The purpose of providing this information on customary and legal norms associated with the family in Sierra Leone is to show how conjugal order is shaped in this country. Both legal and customary practices are patriarchal and prioritize men's rights over women's. Legal marriages are increasingly more attractive to women because only women who enter these forms of marriage have legal claims to property and inheritance. Thus, women are sent the message that they cannot expect certain rights without entering into formalized marriages.

Rape and the Conflict in Sierra Leone

Throughout the conflict, rape, sexual violence, and sexual slavery were primary tactics of warfare. The Truth and Reconciliation Commission report recorded the testimonies of more than 800 women and girls who had been raped, but these represent only a small portion of the total estimated number of victims of sexual violence.[32] Although rape was used throughout the eleven-year conflict, the highest number of incidents was reported during the 1999 rebel incursion into Freetown. Between March 1999 and March 2000, a total of 2,350 rape survivors were registered in Freetown alone during the Rape Victims Programme of the Forum for African Women Educationalists (FAWE).[33] Of these survivors, 2,085 were between the ages of zero and twenty-six years, and 165 were over the age of twenty-seven.[34] It was reported that "many" other victims of sexual violence did not come forward for treatment.[35]

The available statistics and information pertaining to war rape in Sierra Leone paint an overwhelming picture. Physicians for Human Rights (PHR) estimates that between 215,000 and 257,000 girls and women may have been affected by sexual violence in Sierra Leone.[36] It is estimated that between 70 and 90 percent of females abducted during the conflict were raped.[37] The majority of the incidents of sexual violence reported to PHR (68 percent) occurred between 1997 and 1999. Much of the available information about sexual violence in Sierra Leone offers statistics related to particular categories of women, including abducted women, female soldiers, or refugees. For example, throughout the civil conflict in Sierra Leone, research indicates that 50 percent of all female refugees, 75 percent of all females abducted during the conflict, and 75 percent of former girl soldiers, abducted children, and "unaccompanied children" were raped.[38] Categorizing women and girls into particular groups makes it difficult to determine the total numbers who were raped in Sierra Leone—particularly when one considers the likelihood of underreporting due to social stigma and pressure. My own research found that current statistics grossly underestimate the rape statistics.[39] On one occasion, I had access to the intake forms of child soldiers and abducted and unaccompanied children. The data relating to girls between the ages of three and eighteen indicate that thirty-one out of forty-two girls (75 percent) had been raped. Regardless of the precise statistics, one can confidently conclude that sexual violence was a major element of the conflict in Sierra Leone and impacted a significant portion of the population.

Although rape was mainly perpetrated by the RUF, all factions involved in the fighting used it as a tactic of war. Women, men, boys, and girls of all ages were raped, but women, especially girls under seventeen, those thought to be virgins, were targeted in particular. In many instances, girls and women were rounded up by rebels, brought to rebel camps, and then subjected to individual and gang rape. Dehunge Shiaka, program officer for the Ministry of Social Welfare, Gender and Children's Affairs (MSWGCA) in Sierra Leone, summarized this pattern of abuse:

> Of course, you know what happens during the war—the rebel would attack a village and then seize and abduct a group of women or even take over the village. They stayed there for a while. While they are there, they rape. Their aim is to move on and take the capital. So when they move to another area they may take some girls and they may forget about the [previous] girls and concentrate on new, fresh girls.

PHR reported that "in many cases the abductees were gang raped, beaten, starved, tortured, forced to walk long distances carrying heavy loads and told they would be killed if they tried to escape."[40] A report by McKay and Mazurana, focusing on girls in military and paramilitary groups, paints a picture of systemic sexual violence against girls in particular.[41] In the study, all respondents who reported their primary role as being fighters also reported that they were forced to be "wives."[42]

Human Rights Watch's report on war rape in Sierra Leone gives the following dismal summary of abuses:

> Throughout the nine year Sierra Leonean conflict there has been widespread and systematic sexual violence against women and girls including individual and gang rape, sexual assault with objects such as firewood, umbrellas and sticks, and sexual slavery. In thousands of cases, sexual violence has been followed by the abduction of women and girls and forced bondage to male combatants in slavery-like conditions often accompanied by forced labour. These sexual crimes were most often characterised by extraordinary brutality and were frequently preceded or followed by violent acts against other family members. The rebel factions used sexual violence as a weapon to terrorise, humiliate, punish and ultimately control the civilian population into submission.[43]

It is important to note that rape did not occur randomly, nor was it merely a "side effect" of the violent war. Rather, rape was used systematically, strategically, and consistently throughout the conflict. There are numerous accounts of women and girls being abducted and kept as "bush wives" and "sex slaves" (these terms have been used interchangeably in various reports and by various organizations). When Physicians for Human Rights conducted a study among 991 internally displaced women and their family members, it found that 94 percent of respondents had experienced some exposure to war-related violence and 13 percent had experienced war-related sexual assault.[44]

Hebbeh Forster explains the legacies of sexual violence in Sierra Leone:

> In some rural areas the concept of rape has taken on new meaning. Women have been forced to accept that sexual favors have to be given to those who protect them, be they rebels, soldiers or Civil Defence Forces (CDF). They have lost all rights to the privacy of their bodies and the right to say no to unwanted and possibly unsafe sex. They consider rape as what happens in the bush. This may be one of the greatest evils of our war.[45]

Although seemingly random rapes were a part of the conflict, there was also significant evidence of strategic and targeted rape aimed at violating conjugal order. For example, in order to sever young soldiers' ties with their families, and to demonstrate their loyalty to the armed group, some boys and young men were forced to rape their sisters, mothers, and even grandmothers. Women were raped in public and sacred places including mosques and churches.[46] Rebels also raped pregnant and breast-feeding mothers.[47] In addition, sometimes rape was inflicted in front of children, parents, and husbands.[48]

My interviews with women and experts in the field of sexual violence in Sierra Leone also showed a consistent pattern of naming sexual violence victims "bush wives," thereby conflating sexual violence with "taking a woman as a wife." This disturbing trend demonstrates that some men who committed sexual violence saw the act in terms of gaining property and gaining consistent access to a woman's body. In addition, sexual violence created a high degree of stigmatization for the victim, and as will be elaborated further, in some cases rendered her "untouchable" or "unmarriageable." As a result, rape could be seen by perpetrators as a lasting violation of enemy men's property.

Broad Impacts of Rape

In addition to disrupting family norms and creating social disorder, rape was used strategically to impart extensive insecurity and stigmatization. Edward Anague explained some of the lasting impacts of sexual violence:

> One of the most famous commanders is still staying with his bush wives in the eastern part of Freetown. The eastern part is a safe haven. I have family visits and visit families that I know were affected by the war. One of the girls was a bush wife and she told me that she was being held captive but wants to stay with him because she has no alternative—she can't go home. She can't go back. If he can feed her she will stay—even if the relationship is forced.

A tactical advantage to wartime rape is the broader social trauma, indignity, and insecurity associated with the act. These lasting and widespread impacts of rape, not only for victims but also for their communities, ethnic groups, and families, remain largely underexamined within international relations and security studies. Moreover, there is little information about children born as a result of wartime rape and their potential vulnerabilities. Even within so-called alternative or critical approaches to security such as the Copenhagen school, these pervasive yet sometimes invisible sources of insecurity are not recognized. Although wartime rape statistics may be included in descriptions or accounts of a conflict, the legacies of the crime are rarely discussed or prioritized as a source of "post-conflict" insecurity. If the international community is to truly recognize rape as a tool and crime of war, these "collateral damages" of wartime rape must be understood and investigated.

There is a great deal of evidence to support the argument that shame and lasting insecurity resulted from wartime rape in Sierra Leone. Despite the widespread use of rape as a tactic of war, women who are victims of rape are still negatively labeled within their communities, blamed for the assault, and ostracized from their family and community. According to Hamidu Jalloh, a local expert working for the United Nations Development Program, stigma acts as a "double assault" for rape victims; not only must women endure the act of rape itself, but they, and their children, can expect to endure further isolation: "[A woman that has been raped] is a second victim—she suffered twice because of the shame and stigma."[49] Stigma compels women to remain silent about rape and sexual assault. As Jalloh explains, "Very few women will get up and say they are raped."[50]

Therefore, the only reliable statistics on rape in Sierra Leone come from organizations like Médecins Sans Frontières or Physicians for Human Rights when women disclose rape at their clinics. There is no way of knowing exactly how many women in Sierra Leone experienced rape but remained silent. In a study of sexual assault victims conducted by PHR, 65 percent of respondents said that they had reported incidents of sexual violence to another person.[51] Shame and stigma were identified as the main reasons for not disclosing the event. Further, "only 53% of women reported seeking help after the attack."[52]

Despite attempts to keep the experience of rape a secret, some women and girls in Sierra Leone are labeled victims of rape based on their roles during the war, where they lived during the war, if they were abducted, and sometimes even if they are single mothers. Within communities that were particularly targeted and ravaged by rebel forces, almost every woman and girl may have been raped. A social worker explains the result: "There are young men in Freetown who say don't touch a woman from the eastern suburbs because they've all been had."[53] Sulay Sesay, a unit manager for the information and sensitization department of the DDR, described how girls who "went into the bush"—either by choice or by abduction—are ostracized in their communities:

A family may shy away from another family because they know they went into the bush with the rebels. They may have not gone on their own accord but they are stigmatized anyway. When [girls] are in the bush they suffer a lot of moral deprivations. Gang sex and that kind of thing—they rape them. So if there are members of the family that went in the bush—especially girls—there is this line. "Your daughter has gone into the bush—she should not be playing with our daughter," and that kind of thing.[54]

Another form of stigmatization faced by women in Sierra Leone comes from the fact that because rape was widely used as a tactic of war, sexual relationships during the conflict are often assumed to be coerced.[55] As a result, there may be a supposition that single, young mothers or mothers who had children at a very young age were victims of sexual violence. This is particularly true for women who admit to having a relationship with soldiers or rebels during the conflict. This assumption is contested by testimonies from interviewees who explained to me that it was not uncommon for women and men to fall in love during the conflict—even while fighting as soldiers together—and have legitimate, consensual relationships. For example, when Tryphena was interviewed in 2005, she was living with a man who was captured with her by the same armed group. She stayed with the group for six months before escaping and finding her family. Tryphena has a one-and-a-half-year-old child. Although her husband is identified in the community as a former rebel, she sees him as her legitimate husband and plans to stay with him and raise her child with him.[56] Family members and the communities of women and men who formed a relationship during the war may deny the bond, and the children they bear, because the union was not authorized through recognized forms of marriage. Therefore, the institution of marriage has been a significant factor in determining if women will face stigma after the conflict.

Because of the vulnerable situation women and girls found themselves in post–armed conflict, and the prospect of shame and stigmatization, some even married their rape perpetrators. Pressure was put on both perpetrators and victims of rape to marry each other to avoid disgracing their families and communities.[57] Susan Shepler explained that some agencies working in Sierra Leone encouraged girls to marry their former commanders and captors. She maintains: "Marriage somehow solves the problem of reintegration for girls in a way unavailable to boys. No one would suggest that boys formalize their relationship to their erstwhile captors."[58] These marriages further complicate ideas of security. Women who marry their perpetrators achieve personal security, albeit tenuous, not by voicing their rape or "securitizing" rape; rather, they achieve security through remaining silent and reintegrating themselves into established and acceptable social relationships.

The relationship between rape and social disorder clearly has multiple and extensive impacts on women's and girls' ability to remain secure and accepted within war-affected communities. The lasting forms of insecurity and social isolation that are inflicted on victims of rape and their wider community mean that victims of rape largely remain silent. For them, the post-conflict period is not necessarily a time of truth and reconciliation but one of secrecy and concealment. Thus, for women in Sierra Leone, the fear of stigmatization or further marginalization associated with disclosing their rapes results in "security as silence."[59] This insecurity cannot be measured in official conflict statistics, nor can it be addressed without serious consideration of gender hierarchies and power disparities both during and after conflict. As such, conceptualizing the warfare period as a security flash, or even a series of security flashes, and assuming that the post-armed conflict period results in a return to peaceful "normal" politics does not capture multiple and lasting sources of insecurity such as wartime rape.

Forced Marriage and International Law

Forced marriage has been a key focus of the Special Court of Sierra Leone, a court set up by the government of Sierra Leone and the United Nations to try those deemed most responsible for the country's civil conflict. There are four different cases before the court, including members from each of the major warring factions and Charles Taylor, who is being tried in The Hague. The trials against members of the Civil Defence Forces, a paramilitary organization, the Armed Forces Revolutionary Council, and former members of the Sierra Leone Army are complete. The members of the CDF were not accused or charged with any crimes related to sexual violence; however, the AFRC members were accused under Article 2 of the Special Court with rape, sexual slavery, enforced prostitution, forced pregnancy, and other form of sexual violence. These crimes are considered crimes against humanity by the court, along with murder, extermination, enslavement, deportation, and torture.[60]

During the AFRC's trial the crime of forced marriage was introduced as a separate crime against humanity for the first time in an international court. The prosecution sought to make the case that forced marriage should be seen as distinct from sexual violence because it could involve forced labor, forced pregnancy, and abduction. In June 2007 each of the three suspects in the AFRC trial was convicted of acts of terrorism, collective punishment, extermination, murder, rape, outrages upon personal dignity, physical violence, conscripting or enlisting children under the age of fifteen years into armed forces or groups, enslavement, and pillage.[61] The AFRC trials and the subsequent debate about rape, sexual violence, and forced marriage demonstrate ingrained gender norms that constitute conjugal order.

The AFRC accused were not found guilty of sexual slavery or any other form of sexual violence or forced marriage. The trial judges threw out the charges of forced marriage, concluding that there was no need to differentiate forced marriage from sexual slavery. The judges initially found that evidence related to forced marriage overlapped with that related to sexual slavery, rendering it "bad for duplicity."[62] The Special Court declared that "there is no lacuna in the law which would necessitate a separate crime of forced marriage as another inhumane act."[63]

The chief prosecutor for war crimes in Sierra Leone soon made an appeal, claiming that

> forced marriage differs from sexual slavery combined with forced labour and is therefore not duplicitous in that forced marriage entails a conduct over time whereby a man forces a woman into a relationship with all the trappings of marriage, and in which . . . there are obligations in relation to the division of chores and sexual relations in a marriage.[64]

Chief Prosecutor Stephen Rapp also highlighted the long-term impacts of forced marriage: "We talked to women who still feel tied to their 'husbands,' even after the conflict has ended."[65] Rapp's argument indicated that forced marriage involves more than forced sex and can cause multiple forms of insecurity for women and girls.[65]

Other international lawyers such as Michael Scharf and Suzanne Mattler have supported the grounds for this appeal. These lawyers point out that crimes against humanity are defined by the "widespread or systematic nature of an attack, and the fact that it is conducted against a civilian population" and conclude: "From the accounts of the survivors, civilian women and girls abducted from their homes during raids and forced to marry the rebel soldiers who abducted them, it is also clear that forced marriage was a part of that widespread attack, which was carried out against the civilian population."[66]

The Appeals Chamber decided to withhold the existing charges for the convicted AFRC leaders; however, it rendered a landmark decision to recognize forced marriage as a distinct crime against humanity. The Appeals Chamber explicitly recognized forced marriage as a crime against humanity according to the Nuremberg Charter and defined forced marriage as

> a situation in which the perpetrator through his words or conduct, or those of someone for whose actions he is responsible, compels a person by force, threat of force, or coercion to serve as a conjugal partner resulting in severe suffering, or physical, mental or psychological injury to the victim.[67]

It is worth quoting a portion of the trial's ruling at length:

> The trial record contains ample evidence that the perpetrators of forced marriages intended to impose a forced conjugal association upon the victims rather than exercise an ownership interest and that forced marriage is not predominantly a sexual crime. . . . They were often abducted in circumstances of extreme violence, compelled to move along with the fighting forces from place to place, and coerced to perform a variety of conjugal duties including regular sexual intercourse, forced domestic labor such as cleaning and cooking for the "husband," endure forced pregnancy, and to care for and bring up children of the "marriage." . . . The Trial Chamber findings also demonstrate that these forced conjugal associations were often organized and supervised by members of the AFRC or civilians assigned by them to such tasks. A "wife" was exclusive to a rebel "husband," and any transgression of this exclusivity such as unfaithfulness, was severely punished. A "wife" who did not perform the conjugal duties demanded of her was deemed disloyal and could face serious punishment under the AFRC disciplinary system, including beating and possibly death.[68]

The court case against the AFRC perpetrators demonstrates the significance of conjugal order even within international law. The court's initial position that rape and forced marriage were overlapping demonstrates how easily sex and the institution of marriage and the family become conflated. The assumption that forced marriage equals sexual violence implies several troubling lines of logic, including: rape is a form of men "claiming" women as their property, similar to marriage; marriage is a guarantor of men's access to women's bodies; and marital labor is an expected part of the union. The fact that there was resistance by the court to consider evidence of slavery, abduction, and forced pregnancy as separate crimes from sexual violence is a disparaging indication of the lack of will to recognize the multiple sources of gender oppression that occur within the so-called domestic sphere.

Conclusion

Wartime rape has been a part of warfare throughout history. The prevalence of rape during more modern conflicts, including those in Sierra Leone, Bosnia, and the Democratic Republic of Congo, has resulted in an influx of research in the field and an increased focus on wartime rape as an important element of conflict. Despite advances, there is still a need to continue to complicate dominant approaches to, and theorizations of, the use of rape and sexual violence both within and outside of warfare.

During "peace," sex is regulated through marriage and family law. In efforts to disrupt order during conflict, soldiers violate patriarchal norms, which define women and children as property of men, heterosexual sex within marriage as sacred, and the control of women as a signifier of power and masculine identity. Social norms related to the family unit and marriage dictate that marriage is the institution within which sexual relationships are authorized and provide the context against which rape is understood not only as a violation of an individual body but also as a source of individual, family, and community shame. Security and securitization discourse are limited because they assume a gender-neutral intersubjective process of securitization and ignore the significance of relationships and norms predominantly considered "natural" or part of the domestic realm, including sex and the family.

Although this chapter has focused on Sierra Leone, it is important to note that institutionalized patriarchal norms associated with marriage and the family are not exclusive to this country and are relevant both within and outside of war. It would be difficult to find a society in which conjugal order, or ideas and institutions associated with heterosexuality, marriage, childbirth, and the nuclear family, did not inform gender orders. Periods of disorder—such as war—provide a unique opportunity to view the intricate and vast mechanisms of social and political order that are implicated in a "peaceful" society. These mechanisms and complex relationships must inform a feminist understanding of security studies. Furthermore, feminists should not become enticed by tendencies within the field to concentrate on security flashes and abandon efforts to investigate wider social and political contexts. Wartime rape is more than just a brutal side effect of war. It is an indicator of embedded patriarchal assumptions and practices within "normal" and "peaceful" society. Given the length of Sierra Leone's civil war, the sanctioned and extensive use of rape within warfare may be emblematic of the prolonged impacts of militarism and hypermasculinity on shifting conjugal order within the country. Response to wartime rape requires a brave examination of these rooted norms and practices as well as a radical redefinition of insecurity and instability.

7

Loving Your Enemy

Rape, Sex, Childbirth, and Politics Post–Armed Conflict

Kadiatu was with the rebels for one year. She admitted to killing and "holding weapons." At just twenty-two years of age, Kadiatu has three children, aged eleven, seven, and three. This means her first child was born when she was just eleven years old. Kadiatu explained that the children were all born from a rebel and was adamant that they were all fathered by the same man. Kadiatu admits that things are "strange" between her and her children and complained that she had no assistance in parenting. Although Kadiatu did not clarify where the father is—or if he is alive—she said she tells her children their father is dead.[1]

Salamatu thinks she was eighteen or nineteen when she was with the fighting forces. She escaped but still does not know what the DDR is. Salamatu has two children. The first, a four-year-old, was fathered by a rebel. Salamatu did not give any more details other than "he is dead." Her second child, a one-year-old, was fathered by her current husband. Salamatu explained that her husband "doesn't accept" her first child and has insisted the child be raised by Salamatu's mother.[2]

Sara Ruddick has written that "[women's] maternal conception of the history of human flesh sets them at odds with militarist endeavours."[3] Ruddick's work is representative of maternal feminists' conclusions about women's natural aversion to war and conflict. Ruddick has written about the positive impact of motherhood on women and especially how it transforms women's perspectives on ethics, care, and violence. Although Ruddick has admitted that her perspective is a product of her position as a white, heterosexual, Western woman, the limits of this argument have perhaps been underestimated. Associating sex and childbirth as a natural and positive experience for women in Sierra Leone—or many other contexts—is beyond absurd. This presumption about women's natural role and emotions casts a violent, moralizing net over all women in all contexts. Women who do not fit into this mold of the natural, superior, feminized peace-builder are judged, ignored, or rendered delinquent or exceptional. It is perhaps only by exploring women's knowledge of the history of human flesh and their roles within militaristic endeavors that the facade of traditional notions of natural, peaceful mothers might be exposed.

Charles Helwig poignantly wrote, "[Women] know what war is about because war is part of any woman's daily experience. Daughters or sisters or wives, we know about 'loving your enemy' in a particularly direct and painful way."[4] This quotation begins to capture the intricacy of women's roles, relationships, and vulnerabilities during conflict. Moreover, through this quotation, one can begin to consider the assumptions associated with "love" and "enemy." In Sierra Leone, women indeed knew about loving their enemy. In many cases women were raped by a member of their family or community. Thus, a loved one became an enemy. After the official end of the war, a number of women were forced to marry their rape perpetrators, rendering enemies "loved ones." Men and women who may have been part of enemy armed groups sometimes formed legitimate relationships or fell in love. Women who were raped by enemies were expected to love the children who were conceived as a result. Foreign troops and peacekeepers who arrived to protect civilians from "the enemy" also raped both civilians and combatants. In turn, the simple biblical reference of "loving your enemy" acts as a lens through which it becomes possible to see how sex, love, the family, and childbirth are intimately implicated in warfare. This reference also acts as a starting point for this chapter, which aims to examine and rethink both the idea of women as natural mothers and the assumption that sex and childbirth are private—particularly in the context of war.

This chapter is focused on children born as a result of war—children sometimes referred to as "war babies." Building on the previous chapter, which concentrated on wartime rape as a warfare strategy, this chapter supports the argument that the emphasis of "immediate" and "hard" security issues over "everyday politics" has meant that rape as a tactic of war in Sierra Leone and children born as a result of rape are two issues that have largely been pushed to the margins of conflict, development, and security studies. Sex and childbirth have traditionally been considered private concerns, distant from pressing security matters; consequently, a generation of children born as a result of wartime rape has been virtually ignored, despite the fact that both survivors of rape and their offspring may face serious insecurity concerns.

Through existing research as well as my own statistics, I seek to establish children born of rape as a significant population group requiring specific resources and attention. This chapter also discusses the inability of aid agencies to name and categorize children born of war within their existing classifications of vulnerable children–child soldiers, abandoned children, and street children. Not identifying children born of rape as a particular category of vulnerable children in Sierra Leone is a political choice that stems from the misconception that sex and the family are neither a political nor a security issue.

A secondary aim of the chapter is to deconstruct dichotomies associated with mothers and war, such as courageous male warriors and peaceful nurturing women. This analysis draws on Jacqueline Stevens's analysis of the relationship between the state and the family, as well as feminist critiques of representations of "natural" mothers.[5] Lene Hansen's work related to identity formation is also employed in an examination of the consequences for women who do not fulfill the definition of woman as "emotional, motherly, reliant and simple."[6] Hansen has argued that the language used in policies directed at particular groups of people helps shape general ideas and attitudes about them. As a result, policies can serve to construct or obscure particular identities and categories of people. For example, policies that assume women are the primary caretakers of children help reify the stereotype of women as naturally nurturing and part of the so-called domestic sphere.

In the context of larger debates on the naturalness of the family and the liberal tendencies of post-conflict programs, children born of rape are a fascinating case study. By examining the various stigmas attached to children born of rape, it becomes obvious that these children are considered exceptional, although not necessarily because of the rape that produced them; rather, these children are understood as atypical because they defy most understandings of conjugal order. Children born as a result of rape are born as a result of sex outside of marriage or a recognized, "legitimate" sexual relationship; as a result, they challenge the traditional liberal model of the family because they reveal that not all children are considered natural extensions of the family unit.

Conjugal Order and Colonial Rule in Sierra Leone

As mentioned in the introduction, the concept of conjugal order refers to laws and social norms that serve to regulate sexuality, (re)construct the family, and send messages about acceptable and legitimate social relationships. The purpose of this chapter is not to depict a singular version of conjugal order. Instead, the custody, adoption, and paternity laws that influence conjugal order in Sierra Leone are provided. The objective is to show how existing laws, norms, and practices dictate acceptable family structures and determine which children are "legitimate." These regulations create a particular form of conjugal order that renders children born of rape as "unnatural," illegitimate, and a potential source of family shame.

Custody Laws

The customary and civil laws regulating paternity and custody in Sierra Leone are fascinating and complex. One report summarizes the basic premise of these laws:

> Rights over the procreative services of a woman are vested in her paternal family until they are transferred at marriage to her husband and his family. If a girl has a child before marriage, her family, not having transferred these rights to any man, would be in a position to claim damages from the man who has trespassed on their rights and to claim the child. Ideally, of course, in the traditional village society, all women past puberty should be married, thus avoiding such a situation.[7]

As mentioned in chapter 2, although most regulations associated with custody and adoption in Sierra Leone stem from ethnic norms and customs, the Ministry of Social Welfare, Gender and Children's Affairs has increasingly tried to intervene in these areas. Dehungue Shiaka, from the Ministry of Social Welfare, Gender and Children's Affairs, explained that in cases of divorce, the ministry investigates the parents to decide if the father is capable of caring for the child.[8] As noted earlier, in most cases, it deems the mother to be the best possible parent for the child.[9] It is assumed that the mother is "more naturally prepared to mother [sic] children" and that fathers are often too busy working to care for children.[10] In these cases, if the father requests custody of a child after the child reaches the age of ten, custody is usually granted to him.[11] The rationale for this shift from the mother to the father is that, after the age of ten, the child is better able to take care of him- or herself, and the father is more likely than the mother to have the financial resources to further the child's education and provide him or her with various opportunities.[12]

One area of law that is currently under review in Sierra Leone relates to the practice of adoption. Traditionally in Sierra Leone, if a mother cannot raise her child or dies, the biological father's parents will raise the child. Children born during the conflict represent new challenges to this traditional practice. First, children may be born as a result of rape or gang rape. In this case the father may not be known, and there is no relationship or sense of obligation between the father and the child. Second, children may be born as a result of consensual sex during the conflict between an unmarried couple. In this case, the father's family may reject the child as illegitimate because there had been no recognized marriage. Third, the location of the father and his family may not be known either as a result of the mass displacement of the population during the conflict (more than 1 million people were displaced from their homes) or as a result of the high number of deaths during the conflict. After the war there was an increase in the number of women with children who were either unmarried, did not know the father, did not want to locate the father, or had been rejected by the family of the father. However, there were no real legal or customary frameworks to address these situations. In response, after the official end of the war, the Ministry of Social Welfare, Gender and Children's Affairs began creating the Bastardy Act (now called the Adoption Act) to attempt to legally address children born into such circumstances.

The customary and civil laws regulating paternity and custody in Sierra Leone are fascinating and complex. By law and convention, children are the property of males in Sierra Leone. Husbands have the right to acknowledge, as their legitimate child, any offspring born to their wives, regardless of who the biological father is.[13] If a child is born as a result of an affair, the husband legally has what amounts to "first right of refusal." If he does not recognize the child, then the biological father may recognize the child as "his" and register the birth.[14] If neither occurs, then the child falls into legal limbo with respect to inheritance and succession rights.

There is no concept in customary law directly comparable to "legitimacy" within Sierra Leone's legal system. However, according to family law the following cases cover those children whose "legitimacy" is solidified in terms of rights of succession and inheritance:

1. A child born to parents who are legally married.
2. A child fathered by a man other than a wife's husband, but who is explicitly acknowledged by the legal husband as his own.[15]

This short list defining "legitimate" children in Sierra Leone can be contrasted to the long list of categories of children whose paternity, and therefore inheritance and succession rights, can be easily disputed or called into question:[16]

1. An extra-marital child, not acknowledged by its mother's legal husband.
2. Children born to a union that has had the consent of the families, but where dowry and other ceremonial traditions have not been finalised.
3. A child born to a betrothed girl and fathered by the intended husband.
4. A child born to a betrothed girl and fathered by a man other than the man to whom she is betrothed.
5. A child born to a married woman and fathered by her partner in a "caretaker marriage."[17]
6. A child born to a divorced woman and fathered by her partner in a "debtor-creditor marriage."[18]
7. A child born to a widow who has been "inherited" or married by a male relative of the deceased husband, and who has been fathered by another man.
8. A child born to an unmarried girl for whom no marriage has been arranged and who has been fathered by an unmarried man who does not intend to marry the girl.
9. A child born to a married or divorced woman and fathered by a man who neither is nor has been the woman's husband, but who registers the birth of the child as his own.
10. A child whose mother is married by customary law and who has been fathered by her husband whose personal law is customary law, but who is married by statutory law to another woman.
11. A child whose mother is unmarried and who was fathered by a man already married under statutory law.

These laws and regulations surrounding childbirth and paternity determine which children are accepted. Only particular categories of children are classified as innate members of a family unit while other children are deemed exceptions, problems, or challenges to the family. This further supports the argument that the family is not a naturally forming, prepolitical unit; rather, it is constructed and regulated largely through laws and social norms. These laws inform conjugal order in Sierra Leone. Looking at the issue of war babies through the lens of conjugal order provides clarity regarding the social disorder these children present and the inability of aid agencies and organizations to recognize them as a category of vulnerable children.

War Babies

Given the relative silence and inattention to the issue of children born of war, it is exceptionally difficult to confirm their numbers or to learn what has happened to such children after birth. Many women and girls refused to talk about rape, and it was nearly impossible to determine if children abandoned during the war were products of rape. Speaking about an orphanage run by CIS, Rev. Hassan Mansaray noted:

> "In our orphanage it is very difficult to know [if children were products of rape], especially if you have the child as a baby. The child doesn't know how to talk when you get that child so we can't get the history. Even as the child grows it is very difficult even if the single mother or the biological parent knows that that child is hers [they] find it difficult to come out and say that they are the legitimate mother and because of certain situations had to abandon it.

As an afterthought Mansaray added, "We have a few children that were already old enough that saw their parents raped. One girl saw her mother raped and then killed. Another girl, she saw her father's head cut off."

Much of the information I gathered about war babies came in the form of stories told to me by staff at orphanages like Augustan, social workers, or other members of the community in Sierra Leone. Most people who had worked with children during the war knew about this category of children, but few could tell me many specifics about their numbers or their fates. For example, when asked about war babies, Glenis Taylor from UNICEF offered what she knew about these children:

> We were receiving reports of girls who were found abandoned in communities mostly with babies. Some of the abductors abandoned the girls and went back to their original areas, and these girls were ashamed to go back. Most of them had babies—maybe one, two, or three—and a lot of them were hesitant to go back. Life had been difficult before, and now they were going back with an extra mouth or two to feed and they had no skills. Some didn't know if their family was alive, some wondered if the family hadn't looked for them for all this time maybe they don't want them back. They had reservations and insecurities. Some of them were accepted in a new way of life, some left their homes as children and were returning as adults, and for some this worked.

Catherine Zainab Tarawally, director of Human Rights Awareness in Makeni and manager of Radio Maria, reported that "southern and eastern people don't forgive and forget, but the northerners do. These people don't care for these women, some have impregnated women, and they have had two or three children. But after the disarmament these men just go away and leave the children with the women. That's why we have a lot of dropout women in this part of the country after the war."

Rev. Hassan Mansaray from CIS also had some knowledge about war babies:

> The experiences with those children are not very pleasant. For example, the orphanage that we run, we believe some of the children that were abandoned are children associated with rape. Like the first boy we had when we started the orphanage, he was six months when he was thrown away. The issue of rape is something very bitter and something that destroys the integrity of the girls because most people in the community, when they know that a child is born out of such a situation, the child is stigmatized— and also the mother. Those are problems that usually, well, so many people find difficult to realize that the child suffered maybe as the result of ill luck, but they leave the fate of the child.

Information about a particularly detectable category of "war babies" sheds further light on this issue. Children born as a result of rape or consensual sex between Sierra Leonean women and foreign peacekeepers or UN staff are more identifiable because they often inherit distinct physical characteristics. Although some women had consensual relationships with these men, there were also cases of UN staff and peacekeepers committing rape. Furthermore, the use of Sierra Leonean women and girls as prostitutes remains a serious concern. Shiaka admitted: "We had ECOMOG [Economic Community of West Africa Monitoring Group] and the UN, and all of them had relationships with girls and there were children from those relationships."[19] Francis Lahai confirmed Shiaka's analysis by stating, "During the war we had a lot of peacekeeping troops coming and then going back, and around them we used to see a large number of girls, and they had children with these peacekeepers, and they left, and most of these girls have the children with them, and there is no one to take direct control or responsibility. We think this might be a problem for that particular category."

Unable to explain why, Shiaka also noted that if a child is born from a rebel, "the stigma is much more greater [sic] than when a girl has a baby with an ECOMOG soldier or a peacekeeper."[20] This is contradicted by Lahai, who, when asked about the potential stigma for children born of foreign peacekeepers, stated, "Nobody wants to accept a child of that nature. Within the family setting we do not make much difference, but in some cases families reject them."

Whether or not this "ranking" of children born of war favors children born to foreigners, their visibility in the community renders them vulnerable in comparison to those children whose paternity remains hidden. Even if a child experiences less stigma than other children born of war, the issue of abandonment is a real concern for children born from foreign soldiers or staff. For these children there is limited hope of locating their fathers just as there is limited hope for their mothers of receiving help with the child from the family of the father.

Finally, my interviews with female soldiers provide additional information about this category of children. Some women I interviewed were willing to talk about children they had given birth to during the war. I did not specifically ask women if they were raped or if their children were born as a result of rape; however, some women voluntarily disclosed information about children who had been fathered by rebels or by men who had subsequently died. Interestingly, none of the women used the words "rape" or "sexual violence." There seemed to be code phrases that broadly referred to sex but obscured whether the act was forced or not. For example, several women explained that they had been taken as "wives" by one or more men. As already mentioned, the phrase "taking someone as a wife" typically refers to having sex in Sierra Leone. It is not always clear whether this sex is forced or not; however, it is important to note that "bush wife," "wife," and "sex slave" are often used interchangeably by women and are even used this way within organization documents and reports. One female soldier lamented: "Those men [soldiers and rebel] have their own wives to return to without the kids. It was only because of the war that they had these women as their temporary wives."

Also, many women, like Kadiatu and Isatu, referred to their children as "being from the bush." Very few women clarified what they meant by this, although both Kadiatu and Isatu added that their children that were from "the bush" were fathered by rebels. Tryphena admitted that she does not know where the father of her oldest child is. She has two more children from another man whom she now lives with. She divulged the following about the father of her first child: "If I told them their father is from the bush they will feel strange. I will just say they are from the last father." Due to the chaos, displacement and mass movement, and endemic sexual violence that characterized "the bush," the interviewees' use of the term with reference to their children seems to indicate one of a number of possible scenarios: the paternity of the child is unknown, the child was fathered by a man with whom the woman wants no further contact, the woman does not know where the father is anymore, or the father is dead.

My research revealed many cases of women who gave birth during the conflict and later married a man other than the child's father. Twenty-four percent of the women I interviewed acknowledged that they had children born from at least two different fathers. Generally, divorce and remarriage have been quite common in Sierra Leone. The new husband will traditionally adopt his wife's children and formally or informally accept them as his own. But several women interviewed indicated that there were "problems" between their current husbands and the children they had given birth to before the marriage.[21] Unfortunately, due to blanket assumptions about sex and childbirth during the conflict, husbands may reject children born during the conflict as "bad blood."[22]

One woman in particular confided that her mother had to raise the child she gave birth to during the war because her new husband would not accept the child.[23] Another, who had a child "in the bush" and later remarried, told me that she believes her current husband wants to kill her and complained that due to fear "even yesterday I did not sleep all night." Isha Kamara, a social worker with the Girls Left Behind project in Makeni, reiterated that men who marry former soldiers hesitate to accept children they think may have been born as a result of rape. She gave the following details:

> Some men [may think] how should I take this child, they say I won't accept these children because I am not the father of these children. But some husbands they accept because it was because of the circumstances of the war that [women] were involved. Maybe because of threats to this lady...[she got pregnant and] gave birth. [Our organization], we call them and we say war is not a good thing let's forgive and forget. Even the things we have seen, accept the poor children, accept the women.

Abandonment was a consistent theme in the narratives from women who gave birth to children who may be classified as "war babies." Marie told me that her second husband has abandoned her "because he says I have another husband, the rebel. He has abandoned me, and I live with my aunt. I don't want the child to have mixed feelings—I will say that the second father is the father of the two." Hawa had three children, aged eight, three, and one. She said that they all had the same father but that he had left her to go and dig diamonds. He was not providing any support for the children. She added that two of the children were living with her mother, while the youngest had to stay with her because she was still breast-feeding. Fatmata was also raising three children on her own. Alimatu reported that the father of her first child is dead and the father of the second was a rebel. She clarified that the second father abandoned her and her child. When asked what she will tell her children about their paternity, she replied that she planned on telling them the "true story," that one father has abandoned them and the other "died in the bush."

Like Alimatu, Abby intended on being honest with her children regarding their paternity. Abby was with the rebel forces for two years from the age of thirteen to fifteen. She has two children, both of whom were fathered by a rebel who is now dead. She said she will tell her children that their father was a rebel and that they should stay in school. Fatmata explained that the father of her children was also a rebel and that she did not know where he was. When asked what she will tell her children about their father, Fatmata replied, "I will tell them the truth, that their father was a rebel." Another woman, Salamatu, told me she has two children. The father of the first child left her during the war, and she later married a man who fathered a second child. When asked what she will tell her older daughter about her father, she replied, "I give her the real story about the father. But this girl...when she grows up, she will ask me questions, and I will explain more."

Isha Kamara stated that the organization she worked for was actively encouraging women to conceal the paternity of their children. She said it was particularly important for a child not to know that his or her father was a rebel who had committed rape:

> Now we have asked women to stop telling their children that they are a product of rape because that will make the child to be shy, even that will make the child afraid to say they have a father. [We believe] if you are saying that the child is a rebel...that child will not be happy—she cannot say anything about their father at school when the children are saying "my mother gave me this...my father gave me this," so we are telling them talk to the husband and tell the husband to take the child and ask for forgiveness.

Accounts of war babies in countries such as Bosnia, Japan, and Rwanda have noted the tendency for mothers to reject or harm these children. One cannot draw such general conclusions based on information regarding the relationship of mothers to children born of war in Sierra Leone. Mameh Kargbo from COOPI explains the complicated feelings that women might feel toward children born of rape: "Some wanted to take the lives of their children [who were born of rape] they say 'these children are constant reminders. Tomorrow they will ask 'where is my father.' [The women] say that will always remind them. They wonder how they can tell children that they were raped by 4 or 5 men." From her experience working with women, she concluded that for those who have been gang-raped "the agony of not being able to identify the father of their child is sometimes too much to bear."[24] Dehungue Shiaka of the Ministry of Social Welfare, Gender and Children's Affairs also maintains that women will likely have strained relationships with children born of rape:

> There could be social problems on both sides [the mother and the child]. Because on one hand we have a mother that thinks, "ok, this child is my child and I thank the Lord for this child," but on the other hand this child is a product of rape and the mother will think, "the rebel raped me and this is the result." So that kind of normal care that you would expect from a mother may not happen, and if that baby grows up with that kind of neglect from the mother, then the frustration will also be with the baby, and there is a possibility that there will be a bad relationship on both sides from the growing child who may think that the mother is neglecting him or her and the mother too that may think that "oh this child is his [the perpetrator of rape].[25]

In contrast, Glenis Taylor from UNICEF Sierra Leone felt that most of the mothers of children born of rape accepted their children. She told a particularly moving story:

> There was a girl mother in a center and she lost her child. She was not interested in gaining contact with the father. The child died, and I thought she would have been happy with that—poor child—but she cried and was so unhappy. She was saying, "after all this—this was what I had to show at least I had this child as a product of my pain." She was very upset. Many women were interested in having the best for their children.[26]

Very few of the women I spoke with gave detailed information about their relationship with their children. One woman I spoke with admitted that things were not easy between her and the child she gave birth to during the war: "Right now with the children we have some strangeness with them. We gave birth from the rebels, and now we are having problems with them. All the men left the children with the women, and they need some help." Fatmata had also revealed that her relationship with her children was "not easy," but that she cannot linger on the difficulties with the relationship because "they need to be fed and go to school and I'm by myself."

Other information has been gathered from medical intake forms for girl soldiers discovered at CAW. In a group of fewer than fifty girl soldiers, at least six had either recently given birth, were pregnant, or had received an abortion. Ellie was a child soldier with the RUF for one year and five months. In that time she became pregnant, but the pregnancy was aborted at five months, three weeks. Since the abortion she had not received any medical attention. Maya was reported to have been abducted by a SLA soldier called Brigadier Bayo. She gave birth to a baby while in the army (the forms did not indicate who the father was or if the child was the result of rape). Fatmata was a girl soldier who arrived at the CAW facility five months pregnant. According to the reports, her pregnancy was confirmed to be the result of "rape by the SLA boys in the bush."

With such sparse information, it is nearly impossible to know the exact numbers of children born of rape in Sierra Leone. Child welfare experts there could only speak generally about the number of children born of war. Augustan Turai of the Ben Hirsh Society declared: "There are *many* within the community."[27] Rev. Hassan Mansaray said that one of the orphanages his organization works with was established because of the high number of abandoned babies. He estimated that about 20 of the 400 children who went through his facility during the conflict were abandoned babies he believes were born out of rape, or to women who had been abandoned by the child's father.[28] The babies typical ranged in age from six months to just over one year.[29] It is important to note that currently there are no formal mechanisms for identifying and tracking children born of war.

What we do know about war babies is that while sexual violence occurred throughout the eleven-year civil conflict, the majority of rapes were committed between 1997 and 1999.[30] From this it can be inferred that, as of 2012, children born as a result of violence during the war may be between the ages of seven and eighteen years, with the majority of children in the age range of twelve to fourteen. PHR has estimated that 9 to 10 percent of rapes during the conflict resulted in pregnancies. This would mean that more than 20,000 "war babies" might have been born. As noted earlier, rape statistics are extremely skewed in Sierra Leone, and this assessment is therefore a low approximation. While the available numbers may not seem significant, they are likely gross underestimates of the total number of children born of wartime rape. Information about this vulnerable population and means to identify it are crucial to determining the total number these children, as well as assessing their needs.

We also know that most abandoned war babies were fostered or stayed in orphanages because it was impossible to trace their biological families. Augustan Binue explained that due to a lack of resources there was no follow-up on children who were fostered.[31] In a country fraught with poverty, this can result in children growing up in desperate circumstances. Rev. Mansaray reported, for example, that

> most of [the foster families] already had several children of their own—some five or six—so when you place a child with them in the midst of poverty the problem is that the children are mostly used to work. Like three years ago one child was killed along the highway. They sent her to buy wood, and she carried the wood on her head to her house, and they would sell this wood and out of the profits they would feed the family. Some even send the children to the street to sell or to beg for additional income to augment the running of the families. There are few families that can afford the fees to send their children to school.[32]

This testimony sheds light on what life is like in Sierra Leone for children born of war. Far from experiencing a time of development and security post-conflict, these children face multiple insecurities, including poverty, alienation, and abandonment.

Stigma and Children Born of Rape

Unfortunately, stigma does not attach just to the women and girls who have been raped; the children they have given birth to also face similar labeling and stigma. "Rebel baby," "bush pickin" (bush baby), and "banfa baby"[33] are all labels used in Sierra Leone to describe children born of rape. Francis Lahai, who works with the Street Children's Task Force in the MSWGCA, reported as follows: "Community people, whatever the case, say 'oh this girl was missing during the war, she has reappeared with a child—who is the father?'...If it is not possible to know who the father is, they will start stigmatizing the mother and the child and calling them names."[34] Rev. Mansaray from CIS also affirmed: "When [community members] know that a child has been born out of such a situation [rape], the child is stigmatized and also the mother...so many people find it difficult to realize that the child suffered maybe as the result of ill luck."[35]

One factor contributing to stigma is the fact that rape was so pervasive that many single mothers are thought to be victims of rape—whether or not it is true. To remedy this situation, women were readily encouraged to marry either their rape perpetrators or someone who would accept their children. This often meant that children born during the conflict and immediately after had a greater chance of being stigmatized if they are born to a single mother than to a two-parent family—even if their mother was forced to marry her former rebel captor or her rape perpetrator.[36]

Stigmatization is not the only obstacle facing children born of war. Many children—whether or not they are born as a result of rape—have mothers and fathers with limited parenting skills. Their parents may have been involved with the fighting forces from childhood and may never have been parented themselves. This is of particular concern for women and girls because they are typically responsible for child rearing in Sierra Leone. Some girls were abducted at extremely young ages. In particular, 23 percent of the women interviewed in Makeni gave birth before the age of fifteen.[37] Some could not remember life before they were with the fighting forces because they were recruited at such young ages. These girls grew up to be fighters, not mothers. Even women and girls who did not grow up with the fighting forces may lack knowledge about parenting owing to the fact that through displacement or death they were separated from one or both of their parents during the conflict.

During the eleven-year civil conflict, large portions of the general population lost or were separated from at least one parent. Thus, there were numerous social arrangements other than the traditional family structure, including households headed by children or women, grandmothers, aunts and uncles acting as primary caregivers, and children growing up in orphanages or foster homes, or spending extended periods in interim care centers. Despite the multiplicity of arrangements for child rearing that existed during the conflict, one single arrangement has been presented as ideal in the "post-conflict" period, namely, that of biological mothers raising their children. The expectation is that mothers possess the necessary skills to do so. In effect, it is assumed that mothering skills will invoke themselves naturally even in the case of those women and girls with neither experience of nor familiarity with motherhood.

Each source of stigmatization for women and children in relation to wartime rape and the children born as a result correlates to notions of conjugal order, including marriage and the model of the liberal family. If a husband rapes his wife, there is no law or social stigma in Sierra Leone that will distinguish the resultant child as atypical. But a child born as a result of a rape that occurred outside of marriage can be identified as a bastard, a war baby, or a rebel baby (unless the mother marries). Stevens describes this distinction as a by-product of policies that regulate the family: "It is the prerogative of the state to distinguish and hence to constitute the difference between what is profane (sex as "fornication," children as "illegitimate") and what is sacred (sex within marriage, legitimate children)."[38]

The Role of NGOs and International Agencies

There are few programs that address wartime rape as a major obstacle to reintegration and rehabilitation in post–armed conflict Sierra Leone. Organizations like PHR have addressed the medical needs of women who were raped, but long-term programs that offer strategies to help women heal are rare. Even scarcer are programs that address the needs of children born as a result of wartime rape. In fact, of all the organizations and agencies that were established in Sierra Leone after the conflict, not a single one identified children born of rape as beneficiaries. When asked why this category of children had been overlooked, a senior member of the MSWGCA could only say the following:

> It is difficult to identify this group, and we have been sensing something about that. During the war we had a lot of peacekeeping troops coming and then going back, and around them we used to see a large number of girls, and they had children with these peacekeepers, and they left, and most of these girls have the children with them, and there is no one to take direct control or responsibility. We think this might be a problem for that particular category.... When women bring children to orphanages we have tried to find out what has happened that they want to give up their child, and we often find that the father was a peacekeeper or a combatant or someone who is not dead or who has left the country.[39]

Not a single person from any of the children's agencies interviewed could explain exactly why children born of war had not been given specific attention. Some mentioned the funding structure of their agencies, admitting that they were only funded to carry out programs for categories of vulnerable children identified by their donors. As a result, even if organizations identified an urgent need to provide for children born of war, if their donors, some of them foreign-based, had not identified such children as beneficiaries, no funds would be made available. As a result, agencies could only address children born of war indirectly, such as through programs for their mothers. Francis Lahai described the result of this lack of direct funding: "We have some partners that in a rather uncoordinated way offer some form of assistance [to children born of war]. But they are living by chance, just by chance."[40]

With no agencies identifying children born of war as a distinct category, the children in effect become an "un"-category with no specific resources, rights, or protection. Policies have identified other categories of vulnerable children but have excluded and thus delegitimized this category. Augustan Binue of the Ben Hirsh Society admitted: "There was nothing put into place for these children. These children were only taken care of by the Interim Care Centre because they were abandoned on the streets and other places and brought here. Those that we cannot trace their families, we foster them and call them 'community children.'"[41] When asked what happens to these children, Dehunge Shiaka simply replied: "They are left."[42]

Even organizations like the United Nations Children's Emergency Fund, which had extensive resources in Sierra Leone and conducted numerous research programs to assess the needs of children post–armed conflict, did not have any response to children born of war. Glenis Taylor from UNICEF Sierra Leone admitted that the issue did not fit within the organization's agenda because "the war is over. We are looking at vulnerable children, broadly, like street children and girl-mothers."[43] She also confessed to pressure from donors: "They are now saying that the war is over…it is now five years since it is over…it is now time to move away from [any] war associations."[44] Thus it seems as though even with the growing awareness of the number of children born of war and their vulnerabilities, organizations cannot overcome the restrictions of their funding.

The radicalization of development or the conflation of security and development policies provides a partial explanation for this neglect. It is argued here that the linking of development and security has resulted in "traditional" security concerns, such as the disarmament of male combatants having taken precedence over the so-called everyday politics of sex and childbirth. Although rape has been identified as a security interest particular to women, rape is still not considered an issue of "high politics." Hansen explains that matters relating to the security of women often get categorized as individual or human security concerns. She argues that issues relating to human security or individual security are still given lower priority than public "collective" security threats and are relegated to the private realm.[45] The prioritization of security concerns post–armed conflict clearly placed women and "the family" in the private realm in comparison to collective security threats such as organized violence.

The official silence on children born of war in Sierra Leone stands in stark contrast to the overwhelming evidence for the existence of this group of children and the widespread knowledge of the vulnerabilities they face. The aid community did not work at shattering the silence surrounding wartime rape or create acceptance of children born as a result. In fact, by failing to identify children born of war as a vulnerable category, NGOs, aid agencies, and international organizations have been complicit in maintaining gender norms and hierarchies that have categorized rape and childbirth as "private" issues rather than as post–armed conflict development and security concerns.

Initial Recommendations and Conclusions

There is a clear need to expand our understanding of children affected by war beyond the categories of child soldiers, abandoned children, street children, and HIV/AIDS orphans. Although the children in each of these cohorts certainly are vulnerable, they do not encompass the entirety of children who require attention. The recent fixation on child soldiers (read: the image of a young male child holding a gun) has eclipsed the need for research on other categories of children impacted by warfare. This "other" category does not include only children born of rape but also children born to amputees, children with disabilities, and children with inherited drug addictions. These groups are all too often overlooked by post-conflict policies and mainstream Western media.

More broadly, this analysis of sexual violence and "war babies" further demonstrates that sex, marriage, childbirth, and motherhood are regulated rather than natural relationships. It is only when assumptions about the naturalness of heterosexual relationships, marriage, motherhood, and childbirth are abandoned that truly original and progressive thinking and policies can be initiated. To start, childbirth and motherhood should not be viewed by policy makers as equally instinctual. Childbirth may be a biological function, but sex and reproduction do not necessarily occur organically. Furthermore, the desire to be a mother and the skills required to nurture children are not necessarily "hardwired." Most of the practices and policies directed at survivors of rape and mothers of so-called war babies were inspired by liberal notions of conjugal order. These include having grandmothers raise grandchildren to help persuade men that their daughters are worthy of marriage, hiding the paternity of children born of rape, and encouraging women to marry their rape perpetrators. Rather than facilitating a "return to normal," each one of these policies and practices demonstrates the intensity of the effort to create and reinforce conjugal order post-armed conflict.

8

Conclusion

Displacing War Mythology and Developmental Logic

This book began with reference to an image of a young male holding an AK-47. The young man was discussed as symbolic of oversimplified characterizations of chaotic, irrational, and male-driven civil wars in Africa. Perhaps it is fitting now to think about what—if any—iconic images of African women exist. A quick online image search using any combination of "Africa," "war," and "women" will inevitably produce a barrage of pictures of female victims or peacemakers. It is apparent that images of women are primarily used to represent the aftermath of civil war or the devastating effect of war on civilian populations. Two photos are particularly prominent. The first, which shows a half-naked young Sierra Leonean woman sitting propped up on one arm with her legs stretched out and her breasts exposed, was used as part of a campaign to raise awareness about sexual violence across the globe by Integrated Regional Information Networks (IRIN), a service of the UN for the coordination of humanitarian affairs. The IRIN campaign, entitled "Broken Bodies Broken Dreams," featured images from victims of sexual violence that were published and shown in exhibitions in New York, Geneva, and Nairobi.[1] A second image used frequently to represent the civil war in Sierra Leone is of a young woman with either one or both of her limbs amputated. There are multiple versions of this picture used by a variety of actors, from online journals,[2] to university research centers,[3] to foreign policy blogs.[4]

Both of these representations of women have typically been employed to raise awareness about the ways that civilians were impacted and victimized by the civil war. Furthermore, they signal that women's bodies are stained with the legacies of the conflict. The reproduction of these images is one of the political choices that serve to reconstruct women in a distinct ways postconflict. Instead of images of women participating in the conflict, or of former female soldiers graduating from skills training programs or returning to school, or representations of the multiple ways women managed to work and survive in the post-conflict environment, these two images of victimized females dominate.

Certainly, sexual violence and amputation are two phenomena of war that deserve attention and research; however, the manner in which women are used to draw attention to these issues seems contradictory. For example, it is perplexing that campaigners chose an image of a bare-breasted young woman to draw attention to sexual violence, exploitation, and abuse. Furthermore, representations of female amputees evoke shock and sympathy on cue; they also perpetuate a generalized understanding of females as being impacted by war rather than participating in it. In this sense the amputation images are particularly ironic considering that Adama Cut-Hand, a high-ranking female RUF rebel, is largely believed to have initiated and fueled the use of amputations as a weapon of war.

One of the aims of this book is to encourage readers to look beyond not only these iconic images but also other sources of dominant war narratives and myths. These representations were countered with a critical examination of sex, power, and the ways that female soldiers are (re)constructed as gendered subjects through post-conflict policies. Each chapter problematized how we understand both conflict and "post-conflict" by looking at the various types of "conflicts," including sexual violence, gendered ordering, stigmatization, and stereotyping that continue in the so-called post-conflict moment. This analysis uncovered the gendered nature of terms such as post-conflict, rehabilitation, violence, reintegration, and development. It also showed how the emphasis on universalism, objective humanitarianism, and liberal economic development overshadows oppressive and restrictive disciplinary measures that take place in the name of achieving these objectives.

Several broad conclusions can be drawn from the preceding chapters. The first is the conviction that analyses of war that are attentive to individual women's and girls' experiences produce a more complicated understanding of women (who can be both victims and aggressors/agents), of conflict (as consuming of the entire society and extending beyond the official time lines of war), and of the post-conflict period (as a nonspecific time that is potentially as violent or repressive as war). Understanding how women experienced war cannot be determined solely by examining the ways in which they have been victimized. To transform the post-conflict period into a time of possibilities, empowerment, and progress for everyone, women must be included in the policy-making and implementation process. This requires in-depth interviews with women and analyses of their war experiences, as well as concerted and ongoing efforts to allow women to share control and participate in decision making. I have argued that individual experiences and stories should not be categorized as either confirming warfare mythologies and expectations or constituting irrelevant exceptions. War impacts individuals in complex and variable ways. Listening to these multifaceted experiences helps to disrupt dominant—and often oversimplified—narratives of warfare.

Furthermore, listening to individual stories assists in dispelling the representation of warfare as an "event" and the postwar period as a staged process. Often war is depicted as if it is a black box of time and space characterized by chaos, violence, unpredictability, and exceptionality, while—in contrast—the postwar moment is seen as a sterile and phased process that can be predictably managed. Post-conflict has almost become understood as a sort of formula: peace accord + disarmament + transitional justice = healing, forgiveness, and harmony. What is missing from this equation are individual experiences. A young woman from Makeni raising a baby born as a result of rape will presumably experience "post-conflict" differently than an orphaned child in Freetown or an HIV-positive teenager from Bo. Recovery, healing, acceptance, and reintegration are personal experiences that cannot be systematized.

When I visited Sierra Leone at the end of 2005, I was certainly given the impression that the international donor community had decided that "the postwar" period was over for Sierra Leone. The reintegration phase of the DDR had long since been finalized for adults, with the children's process ending in December 2005. These programs were ending not because local organizations had declared the reintegration process complete and a success but because donor funding had effectively dried up. In fact, several social workers and community members expressed their concern to me about the abrupt end to the reintegration process. Some told stories of young soldiers whose school fees would cease to be covered; others mentioned the numerous soldiers who had not been included in DDR processes and were unemployed and desperate.

Of the few centers that were offering skills training for female soldiers, the majority were either in the process of ending their programs or struggling to raise money to continue their efforts. On a sweltering day in December I attended a graduation for a class of former female soldiers who had been trained as tailors. In previous years each graduate would receive a sewing machine and a start-up kit with some fabrics, needles, and scissors; however, this year, due to a lack of funding, only the top student received a used machine. Amid expressions of joy and celebration at the ceremony, students and parents expressed concern that the graduates would not be able to generate enough business with their skills to earn a living.

Another program nearing the end of its funded mandate was the National Commission for War Affected Children (NACWAC). The remaining staff at NACWAC indicated that their missions to repatriate refugee children and assist former child soldiers in rehabilitating and reintegrating into their communities were far from complete. Despite the needs within the community for its services, NACWAC had lost the majority of its funding and was no longer considered an essential branch of the Sierra Leone government. Similarly, one UNICEF staff member admitted that even though that organization was still working to reintegrate child soldiers, it had to rename most of its initiatives. Under pressure to move away from war and postwar policies and references, it was now focusing primarily on street children—even if many of those street children happened to be child soldiers.

There were also generalized concerns about the security vacuum that would be created when the majority of the remaining UNAMSIL peacekeepers withdrew in December 2005. Many expressed fear that the local police did not have the competency or resources to sustain social order after a withdrawal. The economic impacts of UNAMSIL's withdrawal were perhaps of even greater concern to many Sierra Leoneans I spoke with. For years UNAMSIL had been one of the largest employers in the country; furthermore, UN staff injected American dollars into the economy. By the end of 2005, several restaurants, clubs, and beaches that were once full of UN and INGO staff—as well as other internationals—were markedly quieter. Witnessing the declared end of the post-conflict phase in Sierra Leone was an eye-opening experience that raised many questions for me about development and post-conflict as an industry. International organizations and the UN not only were concluding programs in Sierra Leone but also were gearing up for work in other war-torn areas. In fact, many of the UN staff that I met in Freetown moved directly from Sierra Leone to Sudan to join a growing mission there, focused on order and reconstruction.

When asked about the impact of war on civilians, Foday Sankoh, a former RUF commander, responded that when two elephants are fighting it is the grass that suffers. This is one viewpoint I share with Sankoh. I believe that if you want to see the impact of war on people—children, women, or men—you cannot only examine the "official" and public conflict and the warring parties. Rather, you must also consider the impact on civilians and communities not only during the war but years later. Mere written descriptions or statistics accounting for deaths and destruction in war tell only one story about conflict; they cannot convey the breadth and depth of various extended impacts of trauma, displacement, horror, and violence on a population. I have argued that a more nuanced and textured analysis comes from speaking and listening to girls and women whose lives are impacted by the conflict, and taking into account their voices and experiences, as well as their views of what needs to be done in order to move forward after war.

A second foundational message this book conveys is that sex, marriage, childbirth, and the body are not private matters to be separated from international politics. From the outset—including a historical analysis in chapter 2 that focused on colonial and postcolonial sexual regulation and its legacies—the concept of conjugal order has been utilized to demonstrate that political policy and power structures depend on and reinforce a particular gendered order. An understanding of conjugal order is also helpful in illustrating the significance of victim characterization for women in post-conflict Sierra Leone. I argue that most iterations of conjugal order assume weak and passive female subjects. This presumption requires and justifies the existence of the male head of household, the male aggressor and protector, and reinforces stereotypes about women as caretakers and natural parents. As shown in chapter 3, powerful and violent women who act and make choices during war disrupt conjugal order because they weaken the imaginary of the damsel in distress and delegitimize the construction of warriors, soldiers, and rebels as exclusively male subjects.

Similarly, attention to conjugal order results in a unique perspective on sexual violence and its legacies. In chapter 6 I argue that rape is an effective tool of war because of established patriarchal order. The act of rape disrupts very particular relationships and norms associated with conjugal order, including the presumption that sex within marriage is sacred; the belief that wives are the property of their husbands and are the containers of family honor; and the conviction that ethnicity, national identity, and community membership are passed on only through the father. Without these norms wartime rape would still be an act of violence, and victims of this violence would be deeply impacted; however, these norms elevate rape from a single act of violence against another individual to one that shames entire communities, negatively brands the victims and any offspring born as a result, and generally wreaks havoc on families and communities.

In turn, conjugal order can be used as a tool to systematically examine how particular understandings of sex, marriage, and the family inform and influence international politics. For decades feminists have been calling for attention to the private sphere; however, this term can obscure the concrete social norms and hierarchies it aims to represent. When anything deemed "below" domestic politics or anything associated with the home, sex, or the family becomes universally obscured and blanketed by this vague notion of "the private," it becomes nearly impossible not only to examine the particulars of these relationships but also to understand their significance to international politics. More precisely, for this book the concept of conjugal order was useful in illustrating the linkages between development and security policies and the ways both rely on, and enforce, a particular form of conjugal order. I have argued that policies directed at enhancing security or development tend to require and institute specific—often Western-liberal—forms of conjugal order.

I have also argued that one should not accept at face value the benevolent, progressive, and universalistic messages perpetuated by development policies. Development actors are not apolitical but have significant powers in shaping and constraining politics, identity, and power structures. Development projects within Sierra Leone reflect trends within the policy and academic field in their presumption of legitimate subjects, behaviors, and values. Through my analysis of post-conflict development programs such as disarmament, empowerment, and reintegration programs I conclude the development project is not about facilitating any forms of so-called indigenous growth, progress, or recovery; instead, these policies presume, promote, institute, and enforce a very particular Western, liberal, capitalist, and patriarchal order. Moreover, development policies do not necessarily replace traditional, corrupt, chaotic, or violent arrangements with peaceful and progressive ones.

In war-torn areas of Africa in particular, international development programs are often depicted as rescue missions for regions that are too devastated and chaotic to initiate their own recovery. It took only a few interviews to determine that this approach to development is naive and condescending. I thought it would be fitting to highlight the recommendations of a couple of people who have worked in the area of development in Sierra Leone for more than twenty years. The first, Hamidu Jalloh, is a Sierra Leonean living in Freetown who has been working in the area of development for most of his career. He expressed his frustration with the disarmament process in Sierra Leone and offered these suggestions:

> This is the way I would have looked at the DDR [disarmament, demobilization, and reintegration] program, if I had my say I would have loved the DDR to be heavily rural biased because most of the people came from

there. We need a heavy investment in infrastructure. There is also a need to work the land resources—the land is lying there, there is wastage nobody knows how to process. We need to offer useful and practical skills training such as farm husbandry. People get frustrated because they can't get jobs with their skills training so they end up going to the diamond mines. Most of the former combatants are in Kono in the mining areas.[5]

Jalloh's suggestions show the need for truly "bottom-up" ideas of development. For him, impractical development initiatives take funding and energy away from programs that could more optimally benefit local areas. Edward Anague, the founder of a small development organization in Freetown that focuses on amputees and victims of sexual assault, offers a second perspective:

We need something that creates employment. If you train for only six months and you can't even fix a button what can you call that person—not a seamstress. Education refocuses. There is a need to give ex-combatants something meaningful so that the person can see it as a legitimate option. This should be a long-term process. It is not a crash course. It is not about giving $100 to ex-combatants. If you wants results it has to be more than a six-month program—NGOs are pressured to produce "results" but in the end the projects don't amount to anything.[6]

Anague reiterates the frustration expressed by Jalloh with short-term inappropriate development initiatives. Similarly, one of the female soldiers I interviewed summed up many of the conclusions of this book in the following short comment. When asked about the DDR and its limitations, she responded:

They disarmed most of the boys and the ladies remained. So when they disarmed boys and men . . . they went back to their different places and they left the women here. . . . The men have gone back to their lives without taking the women with them or the children. They don't say "come with me to start a new life," they just go. . . . So [the organizers of the DDR] need to do something for the women too.[7]

All three responses demonstrate that Sierra Leone does not need projects, models, and plans for development invented from outside its borders; rather, people who live and work in Sierra Leone, who have been impacted by war, who are committed to the country, and who understand the sociopolitical context already possess ideas and plans for progress and change.

I also contend throughout the book that the very definitions of post-conflict and development require critical reexamination. "Post-conflict," "reintegration," "rehabilitation," and "reconstruction" are not gender-neutral terms. In the collective, universal processes that are implemented after the official end of a war, the development, reconstruction, and rehabilitation processes often exclude women and girls. My analysis of the disarmament process and sexual violence demonstrates that for countless women in Sierra Leone, post-conflict reintegration is defined by silence, concealment, stigma, and fear. For them, this period has not always been a time of positive transformation. Hardly a time of progress and empowerment, for all intents and purposes purposes there is no "post-conflict" for many female soldiers in Sierra Leone. For a large number of the women interviewed, different forms of violence such as forced marriage, sexual exploitation, and isolation continue despite the cessation of formal conflict. In addition, female soldiers' social and political choices seem as constrained by notions of loyalty, duty, and identity in the "post-conflict" period as they were during the conflict.

Another overarching conclusion has been that the merging of development and security—or the radicalization of development—exacerbated the tendencies of policy makers to ignore or deprioritize gender as an important variable, and women as immediate concerns. The resistance to naming female soldiers as soldiers discussed in chapter 3 and the categorization of sexual violence and "war babies" as private issues demonstrated in chapters 6 and 7 support the argument that matters including or relating to women during and after war are seldom recognized as policy priorities. In the first instance, policy makers refused even to acknowledge female soldiers as legitimate subjects. In spite of ample evidence that women and girls participated as soldiers during the conflict, policy makers consistently reconstructed and recategorized them either as "wives," "camp followers," or "sex slaves" or as exceptions. Thus, I have concluded that even when women participate in the activities of "high politics" or sectors traditionally categorized as security priorities such as war, they get recast out of the public political sphere and into the domestic realm through post-conflict development policies.

In terms of sexual violence, I have argued that despite the widespread use of wartime rape and the prevalence of children born of such rape, policy makers continued to view sex and childbirth as private issues. Currently, addressing wartime sexual conduct and its impacts is not readily identified as being integral to the restoration of sustainable peace. The disarmament process, which was given top priority, should be concerned with managing sexual violence and the lasting impacts of wartime sexual behavior as much as it is concerned with soldiers surrendering any weapons they may have used during the war.

An additional broader conclusion to be drawn from this analysis is that while the academic field of development has expanded—with a surge in critical, postcolonial, and feminist scholars in particular—development policies have not detached themselves from their liberal influences and modernization tendencies. The dominant discourses of development policy, including the prevalence of development models and the focus on "stages," deliverables, outputs, and capacity, are demonstrative of the liberal bias of development policy as well as continuities with its colonial and imperial roots. Development policy needs its own rehabilitation process. Rather than another reinvention of development policy through discursive incarnations such as participation, empowerment, or capacity building, I argue that radical rethinking of the liberal and imperial roots of development is required. Development organizations cannot continue to reinvent themselves as a sort of humanitarian messiah without taking seriously the multiple failures and limits to current development logic. The gap between scholars who conduct research and provide reflections on issues pertaining to development and the major decision makers in development policy remains far too vast.

In addition, there is a need to revisit the current conceptualization of gender in policy discourses. Equating gender with "women's issues" allows patriarchy to come in through the back door (to borrow a phrase from Christine Sylvester); rather than development actors critically thinking through gender as an analytical category and considering the ways in which their institutions and approaches might reinforce specific gender norms and stereotypes, gender becomes exclusively linked to "women." In turn, this conflation of gender and women removes the responsibility of organizations and policy makers to account for their role in the construction of masculinity and femininity. The result is that both gender and women remain at the periphery as a "special" subcategory of development issues.

In terms of future research, I hope this work demonstrates the need to critique dominant notions of conflict and post-conflict and encourages long-term and in-depth analysis of the impacts of war that take gender and the experiences of women seriously. Feminists should be at the forefront of research that serves to deconstruct and disrupt some of the stereotypical binaries that continue to limit international relations, including victim/warrior, violent/peaceful, and aggressive/maternal. Feminists must resist the temptation to fall into orthodox approaches and understandings of international relations. Specifically, feminist approaches to security should not consist of "women and security," "women and war," or "women and guns." Similarly, feminist approaches to development must move beyond attempts to add women into existing frameworks and programs. Such efforts merely reinforce existing paradigms and discount generations of feminist scholarship that has encouraged a shift in attention away from limited understandings of so-called high politics. Instead, feminist scholars must consistently resist and counter conventional understandings of security and development by paying attention to the ways in which traditional understandings of security and development rely on and enforce explicit forms of gender order.

NOTES

CHAPTER 1

1. For examples of such images, go to worldvision.com.au/.../S2_4_Rights.jpg, www.gendercide.org/case_conscription.html, news.bbc.co.uk/2/hi/africa/2994096.stm, or www.mylearningspace.net.au/.../34/Figure-14.jpg. In fact, the image found at users.otenet.gr/~tzelepisk/yc/cs.htm of a twelve-year-old boy soldier can be seen on multiple sites and campaign posters, including the Children and War: Impact Project at the University of Alberta.
2. Malinda Smith, *Beyond the African Tragedy* (Aldershot: Ashgate, 2006).
3. I develop this concept and discuss its theoretical foundations later in this chapter.
4. For example, see former British prime minister Tony Blair's speech from October 2, 2001, to the Labour Party annual conference, in which he declared, "The starving, the wretched, the dispossessed, the ignorant, those living in want and squalor from the deserts of Northern Africa to the slums of Gaza, to the mountain ranges of Afghanistan: they too are our cause."
5. Disarmament, demobilization, and reintegration (DDR) programs are an example of this. Similar models of this program were used by the Untied Nations in Mozambique, the Democratic Republic of Congo, Sierra Leone, and Liberia.
6. Mark Duffield, *Global Governance and the New Wars: The Merging of Development and Security* (New York: Zed Books, 2001); Mark Duffield, "Social Reconstruction and the Radicalization of Development: Aid as a Relation of Global Liberal Governance," *Development and Change* 33, no. 5 (2002): 1049–1071.
7. Duffield, *Global Governance and the New Wars*, 2.
8. Ibid., 16.
9. Ibid., 11.
10. Ibid., 88.
11. Shadd Maruna and Russ Immarigeon, eds., *After Crime and Punishment: Pathways to Offender Reintegration* (Portland. OR: Willan, 2004), 6.
12. Ibid., 5.
13. Ibid.
14. Isobel McConnan and Sarah Uppard, *Children Not Soldiers: Guidelines for Working with Child Soldiers and Children Associated with Fighting Forces* (Save the Children), http://www.reliefweb.int/library/documents/2002/sc-children-dec01.htm.

15. National Committee for Disarmament, Demobilization and Reintegration, *The DDR Program: Status and Strategies for Completion* (Freetown, Sierra Leone: Government of Sierra Leone, 2002), http://siteresources.worldbank.org/SIERRALEONEEXTN/ Resources/ddr_status.pdf.
16. Susan McKay and Dyan Mazurana, *Where Are the Girls? Girls in Fighting Forces in Northern Uganda, Sierra Leone and Mozambique: Their Lives during and after War* (Montreal: Rights and Democracy, 2004).
17. Susan R. McKay, "The Psychology of Societal Reconstruction and Peace: A Gendered Perspective," in *The Women and War Reader*, ed. Lois Lorentzen and Jennifer Turpin (New York: NYU Press, 1998), 348–362.
18. Mary Caprioli and Mark A. Boyer, "Gender, Violence, and International Crisis," *Journal of Conflict Resolution* 45, no. 4 (2001): 503–518.
19. McKay, "The Psychology of Societal Reconstruction and Peace," 356.
20. Barry Buzan, Ole Wæver, and Jaap De Wilde, *Security: A New Framework for Analysis* (Boulder, CO: Lynne Rienner, 1998).
21. Barry Buzan and Ole Wæver, *Regions and Powers: The Structure of International Security* (London: Cambridge University Press, 2003).
22. Rita Abrahamsen, "Blair's Africa: The Politics of Securitization and Fear," *Alternatives: Global, Local, Political* 30, no. 1 (2005): 68.
23. Lene Hansen, *Security as Practice: Discourse Analysis and the Bosnian War* (London: Routledge, 2006), 35.
24. Selected contributions to the field of gender and conflict include Laura Sjoberg's book *Gender, Justice, and the Wars in Iraq: A Feminist Reformulation of Just War Theory* (Lanham, MD: Lexington Books, 2006); Charli Carpenter's *Innocent Women and Children: Gender, Norms and the Protection of Civilians* (Aldershot: Ashgate, 2006); and Christine Sylvester's "The Art of War/The War Question in Feminist IR," *Millennium Journal of International Studies* 33, no. 3 (2005): 855–878.
25. Rawwida Baksh-Soodeen and Linda Etchart, *Women and Men in Partnership for Post-conflict Reconstruction: Report of the Sierra Leone National Consultation, Freetown, Sierra Leone 21–24 May 2001* (London: Commonwealth Secretariat, 2002).
26. Christine Sylvester, *Feminist International Relations: An Unfinished Journey* (Cambridge: Cambridge University Press, 2002); Laura Sjoberg and Caron Gentry, *Women, Gender, and Terrorism* (Athens: University of Georgia Press, 2011); Swati Parashar, "Feminist International Relations and Women Militants: Case Studies from Sri Lanka and Kashmir," *Cambridge Review of International Affairs* 22, no. 2 (2009): 235–256; Myriam Denov, "Girls in Fighting Forces: Moving beyond Victimhood" (Montreal: CIDA, 2007), http://www.crin.org/docs/CIDA_Beyond_forces.pdf.
27. Christine Sylvester and Swati Parashar, "The Contemporary 'Mahabharata' and the Many 'Draupadis': Bringing Gender into Critical Terrorism Studies," in

Critical Terrorism Studies: A New Research Agenda, ed. Richard Jackson, Marie Breen Smyth, and Jeroen Gunning (New York: Routledge, 2009), 178–193.
28. Denov, "Girls in Fighting Forces."
29. Rachel Brett, "Girl Soldiers: Challenging the Assumptions" (Quaker United Nations Office), http://www.quno.org/geneva/pdf/Girl_Soldiers.pdf; Yvonne Keairns, "The Voices of Girl Child Soldiers" (Quaker United Nations Office, October 2002), http://www.quno.org/newyork/Resources/QUNOchildsoldiers.pdf.
30. Tsjeard Bouta, "Gender and Disarmament, Demobilization and Reintegration: Building Blocs for Dutch Policy" (Conflict Research Unit, Netherlands Institute of International Relations, March 2005), http://www.oecd.org/dataoecd/50/58/35112187.pdf.
31. McKay and Mazurana, *Where Are the Girls?*; Dyan Mazurana and Khristopher Carlson, *From Combat to Community; Women and Girls of Sierra Leone* (Cambridge, MA: Women Waging Peace, 2004); Rachel Brett, "Girl Soldiers: Denial of Rights and Responsibilities," *Refugee Survey Quarterly* 23, no. 2 (2004): 30–37.
32. Specifically, see Christine Sylvester, "Development Studies and Postcolonial Studies: Disparate Tales of the 'Third World,'" *Third World Quarterly* 20, no. 4 (1999): 703–721; Laura Sjoberg and Caron E. Gentry, *Mothers, Monsters, Whores: Women's Violence in Global Politics* (London: Zed Books, 2007); Cindy D. Ness, *Female Terrorism and Militancy: Agency, Utility, and Organization* (New York: Routledge, 2008).
33. Edward W. Said, *Orientalism* (New York: Vintage, 1979).
34. Gayatri Chakravorty Spivak, "Can the Subaltern Speak?" in *Marxism and the Interpretation of Culture*, ed. Cary Nelson and Lawrence Grossberg (New York: Grossberg Books, 1988), 271–313.
35. Ibid., 306.
36. Michel Foucault, *The History of Sexuality: An Introduction* (New York: Random House, 1978).
37. Ibid., 178, 154.
38. Ibid., 25–26.
39. Ibid., 108, 37.
40. Ibid., 111.
41. Jacques Donzelot, *The Policing of Families* (London: Hutchinson, 1979), xx.
42. Ibid., 69.
43. Ibid., 58.
44. Fiona Fox, "New Humanitarianism: Does It Provide a Moral Banner for the 21st Century?" *Disasters* 25, no. 4 (2001): 275.
45. Gilles Deleuze, "Foreword," in *The Policing of Families* (London: Hutchinson, 1979), xvi.
46. Fox, "New Humanitarianism," 284.
47. Jacqueline Stevens, *Reproducing the State* (Princeton: Princeton University Press, 1999), 210.
48. Ibid., 22.
49. Ibid., 218.

50. This work is not anthropological. I do not pretend to know how conjugal order is understood within specific ethnic groups and communities in Sierra Leone. Where possible, I provide as much information as I can related to local practices and norms, marital laws, and paternity laws, but this work is primarily focused on how external—Western-liberal—notions of conjugal order have been imposed within Sierra Leone.
51. In this book I use the expression "children born as a result of wartime rape" to refer to this specific category of children whose paternity is known to be linked to rape. I also use "children born of war" to refer to a larger population of children that may face similar stigmas and vulnerabilities to children produced during rape. Similar to Carpenter's *Innocent Women and Children*, I argue that terms such as "war babies" and "rape babies" are negative and feed the tendency to sensationalize their identity.
52. Hansen, *Security as Practice*, 18–19 (emphasis in original).
53. Stevens, *Reproducing the State*, 23.
54. Judith Butler, *Gender Trouble* (New York: Routledge) 1990; Michelle Lazar, *Feminist Critical Discourse Analysis: Gender, Power and Ideology in Discourse* (London: Palgrave, 2007).
55. Lazar, *Feminist Critical Discourse Analysis*, 4.
56. Ernesto Laclau and Chantal Mouffe, *Hegemony and Socialist Strategy: Towards a Radical Democratic Politics* (London: Verso, 2001).
57. Allan Dreyer Torfing, "Introduction," in *Discourse Theory in European Politics*, ed. David R. Howarth and Jacob Torfing (New York: Palgrave Macmillan, 2005).
58. This includes an analysis of Sierra Leone's marriage and adoption laws and an analysis of government policies related to the disarmament process and marriage and childbirth.
59. These include the policy documents from organization such as COOPI, CAW, Human Rights Watch, CEDA, and Caritas Makeni.
60. More than twenty local languages are spoken in Sierra Leone.
61. See chapter 2 for more detailed information.
62. Exceptions to this include McKay and Mazurana, *Where Are the Girls?*, but many of their interviews are with girl soldiers and not adult women.
63. Macartan Humphreys and Heremy Wienstein, *What the Fighters Say: A Survey of Ex-Combatants in Sierra Leone*, PRIDE Interim Report (June–August 2003).
64. C. Adler and A. Worrall, eds., *Girls' Violence: Myths and Realities* (Albany: State University of New York Press, 2004), 83.

CHAPTER 2

1. Kriole poem, "For Dear Father Land."
2. R. Kaplan, "The Coming Anarchy: How Scarcity, Crime, Overpopulation and Disease Are Threatening the Social Fabric of Our Planet," *Atlantic Monthly* 273 (1994): 44–74.

3. Several useful and insightful texts on Sierra Leone's civil conflict include John Hirsh's *Sierra Leone: Diamonds and the Struggle for Democracy* (Boulder, CO: Lynne Rienner, 2001); Ibrahim Abdullah's *Between Democracy and Terror: The Sierra Leone Civil War* (Oxford: Council for Development of Social Science Research in Africa, 2004); and David Keen's *Conflict and Collusion in Sierra Leone* (New York: Palgrave, 2005). Perhaps the most thorough text is Lansana Gberie's *A Dirty War in West Africa: The RUF and the Destruction of Sierra Leone* (Bloomington: Indiana University Press, 2005). Gberie was a journalist in Sierra Leone from 1991 to 1996 and visited the country for extended periods in 1999, 2001, and 2002. He interviewed many of the major players in Sierra Leone's conflict, including RUF leader Foday Sankoh, former president Alhaji Ahmad Tejan Kabbah, and numerous civilians. Lansana Gberie, Ian Smillie, and Ralph Hazleton also cowrote *The Heart of the Matter: Sierra Leone, Diamonds and Human Security* (Ottawa: Partnership Africa Canada, 2000). This manuscript was published in 2000 during a time of increased scrutiny of the diamond industry and, particularly, the role of "blood diamonds" in fueling, sustaining, and intensifying the conflict, this report on the role of diamonds in the Sierra Leone civil war received a great deal of public attention.
4. Smillie, Gberie, and Hazleton, *The Heart of the Matter*.
5. A. B. Zack-Williams, "Child Soldiers in the Civil War in Sierra Leone," *Review of African Political Economy* 28, no. 87 (March 2001): 73–82; Michael G. Wessells, *Child Soldiers: From Violence to Protection* (Cambridge: Harvard University Press, 2006); R. Maclure and M. Denov, "'I Didn't Want to Die So I Joined Them': Structuration and the Process of Becoming Boy Soldiers in Sierra Leone," *Terrorism and Political Violence* 18, no. 1 (2006): 119–135.
6. There are also several manuscripts focusing specifically on the role of the United Nations and Britain in Sierra Leone, including Assefaw Bariagaber, "United Nations Peace Operations in Africa: A Cookie Cutter Approach?," *Journal of Third World Studies* 23, no. 2 (2006): 11–29, and Paul Williams, "Fighting for Freedom: British Military Interventions in Sierra Leone," *Contemporary Security Policy* 22, no. 3 (2001): 140–168. Despite the detailed accounts of the various phases of the civil conflict offered in these texts, none of them dedicate significant attention to female combatants.
7. Jacqueline Knörr, "Female Secret Societies and Their Impact on Ethnic and Transethnic Identities among Migrant Women in Freetown, Sierra Leone," in *Women and Migration: Anthropological Perspectives*, ed. Jacqueline Knörr and Barbara Meier (New York: St. Martin's Press, 2000), 80–99.
8. Ibid.
9. Fr. Joseph Momoh, interview by author, Freetown, Sierra Leone, December 2005.
10. Catherine Zainab Tarawally, interview by author, Freetown, Sierra Leone, November 2005.
11. Fr. Joseph Momoh, interview by author, Freetown, Sierra Leone, December 2005.

12. Ibid.
13. Ibid.
14. Knörr, "Female Secret Societies," 85.
15. The World Health Organization has identified female genital mutilation (FGM) as a major health concern. Specific groups aimed at stopping FGM and raising awareness include FORWARD, Care2, and the FGM National Clinic Group.
16. John L. Hirsch, *Sierra Leone: Diamonds and the Struggle for Democracy* (Boulder, CO: Lynne Rienner, 2001).
17. Richard Phillips, *Sex, Politics and Empire: A Postcolonial Geography* (Manchester: Manchester University Press, 2006), 119.
18. Ibid.
19. Adekeye Adebajo and David Keen, "Sierra Leone," in *United Nations Interventionism 1991–2004*, ed. Mats Berdal and Spyros Economides (New York: Cambridge University Press, 1996), 246–247.
20. A. Porter, *Creoledom* (London: Oxford University Press, 1963), 3.
21. Adebajo and Keen, "Sierra Leone."
22. Gberie, *A Dirty War in West Africa*.
23. Ibid., 18–19.
24. In ibid.
25. Phillips, *Sex, Politics and Empire*, 2.
26. Lenore Manderson, "Colonial Desires: Sexuality, Race, and Gender in British Malaya," *Journal of the History of Sexuality* 7, no. 3 (January 1997): 373.
27. Mariarosa Dalla Costa, *Paying the Price: Women and the Politics of International Economic Strategy* (New York: Zed Books, 1995).
28. R. C. Harris, "The Simplification of Europe Overseas," *Annals of the Association of American Geographers* 67, no. 4 (1977): 469–480.
29. Quoted in Phillips, *Sex, Politics and Empire*, 1.
30. Ibid.
31. Ibid., 127.
32. Ibid., 128.
33. Michael Crowder, *West Africa under Colonial Rule* (Evanston, IL: Northwestern University Press, 1968).
34. Richard Burton, *To the Gold Coast for Gold: A Personal Narrative* (London: Chatto and Windus, 1883), 187.
35. Quoted in Phillips, *Sex, Politics and Empire*, 182.
36. Lynn M. Thomas, "Imperial Concerns and 'Women's Affairs': State Efforts to Regulate Clitoridectomy and Eradicate Abortion in Meru, Kenya, c. 1910–1950," *Journal of African History* 39, no. 1 (1998): 121–145; Jean Allman and Victoria B. Tashjian, *I Will Not Eat Stone: A Women's History of Colonial Asante* (Portsmouth, OH: Heinemann, 2000).
37. Kristin Mann, *Marrying Well: Marriage, Status and Social Change among the Educated Elite in Colonial Lagos* (Cambridge: Cambridge University Press, 1985), 71.

38. Ernest Graham Ingham, *Sierra Leone after a Hundred Years* (London: Seeley, 1894), 316.
39. Barbara E. Harrell-Bond and Ulrica Rijnsdorp, *Family Law in Sierra Leone* (Leiden: Afrika-Studiecentrum, 1975), 8; quotation on p. 12.
40. Dehunge Shiaka, interview by author, Freetown, Sierra Leone, December 2005.
41. Valerie Nicol, "Promoting Gender Equality through Legal Reform," in *Women and Men in Partnership for Post-conflict Reconstruction: Report of the Sierra Leone National Consultation, Freetown, Sierra Leone 21–24 May 2001* (London: Commonwealth Secretariat, 2002), 59–75.
42. Michael Wessells and Davidson Jonah, "Recruitment and Reintegration of Former Youth Soldiers in Sierra Leone: Challenges of Reconciliation and Post-accord Peace Building," in *Troublemakers or Peacemakers? Youth and Post-accord Peace Building*, ed. Siobhan McEvoy-Levy (Notre Dame: Notre Dame University Press, 2006), 27–49.
43. Kaplan, "The Coming Anarchy."
44. Cooper in Gberie, *A Dirty War in West Africa*, 9.
45. Keen, *Conflict and Collusion in Sierra Leone*.
46. In Barbara Crossette, "Singling Out Sierra Leone, U.N. Council Sets Gem Ban," *New York Times*, July 6, 2000, World section, http://www.nytimes.com/2000/07/06/world/singling-out-sierra-leone-un-council-sets-gem-ban.html.
47. Gberie, *A Dirty War in West Africa*, 85.
48. Adebajo and Keen, "Sierra Leone."
49. Ibid.
50. Abdul K. Koroma and A. N. D. Koroma, *Sierra Leone: The Agony of a Nation* (Freetown: Andromeda Publications, 1996); W. Reno, "The Failure of Peacekeeping in Sierra Leone," *Current History* 100 (2001): 219–225.
51. Ibrahim Abdullah, "Bush Path to Destruction: The Origin and Character of the Revolutionary United Front (RUF/SL)," in *Between Democracy and Terror: The Sierra Leone Civil War*, ed. Ibrahim Abdullah (Oxford: Council for Development of Social Science Research in Africa, 2004), 41–65.
52. In Gberie, *A Dirty War in West Africa*, 93.
53. Paul Williams, "Fighting for Freetown: British Military Intervention in Sierra Leone," *Contemporary Security Policy* 22, no. 3 (2001): 140–168.
54. Adebajo and Keen, "Sierra Leone"; Gberie, *A Dirty War in West Africa*.
55. Adebajo and Keen, "Sierra Leone," 204.
56. William Reno, *Warlord Politics and African States* (Boulder, CO: Lynne Rienner, 1998).
57. Hirsch, *Sierra Leone*.
58. Gberie, *A Dirty War in West Africa*.
59. Adebajo and Keen, "Sierra Leone."
60. Gberie, *A Dirty War in West Africa*, 98.
61. Hirsch, *Sierra Leone*, 150.

62. Ibrahim Abdullah, "Bush Path to Destruction: The Origin and Character of the Revolutionary United Front/Sierra Leone," *Journal of Modern African Studies* 36, no. 2 (June 1998): 203–235.
63. Gberie, *A Dirty War in West Africa*.
64. Williams, "Fighting for Freetown."
65. Gberie, *A Dirty War in West Africa*, 167.
66. Adebajo and Keen, "Sierra Leone," 246.
67. Hirsch, *Sierra Leone*.
68. Thokazani Thusi, "Learning from Sierra Leone," in *A Step towards Peace: Disarmament in Africa*, ed. Nelson Alusala and Thokozani Thusi (Tshwane: Institute for Security Studies, 2004).
69. In Adebajo and Keen, "Sierra Leone," 267.
70. There was a separate disarmament process for children.
71. Reliefweb, "Sierra Leone War Is Over, Declares President 18 January 2002," http://wwww.reliefweb.int/rw/rwb.nsf/AllDocsByUNID/e7837aa561f-4387ac1256b480050a45b (accessed October 12, 2007).
72. Gberie, *A Dirty War in West Africa*.
73. Adebajo and Keen, "Sierra Leone," 215.
74. Isobel McConnan and Sarah Uppard, *Children Not Soldiers: Guidelines for Working with Child Soldiers and Children Associated with Fighting Forces* (Save the Children), http://www.reliefweb.int/library/documents/2002/sc-children-dec01.htm.
75. National Committee for Disarmament, Demobilization and Reintegration, *The DDR Program: Status and Strategies for Completion* (Freetown: Government of Sierra Leone, 2002), http://siteresources.worldbank.org/SIERRALEONEEXTN/Resources/ddr_status.pdf, p. 4.
76. Further details about the DDR process can be found in chapters 4 and 5.
77. As noted in chapter 4, the length of the training programs became shorter as funds for these initiatives dried up. In the end, some ex-combatants were trained for only three to six weeks.
78. Ibid.
79. Ibid.
80. Ibid.
81. For a more detailed analysis of post-conflict training options for female soldiers, see chapter 4.
82. For example, UNICEF's Girls Left Behind program offered *gara* tie-dyeing, catering, tailoring, and weaving. Children Associated with the War (CAW) and the Augustan Bintue organizations offered tailoring for female soldiers.
83. Ibid.
84. Adebajo and Keen, "Sierra Leone."
85. National Committee for Disarmament, Demobilization and Reintegration, *The DDR Program*.

86. Ibid.
87. Ibid.
88. Sulay Sesay, interview by author, Freetown, Sierra Leone, December 2005.
89. Physicians for Human Rights, *War-Related Sexual Violence in Sierra Leone: A Population Based Assessment* (Washington, DC: Physicians for Human Rights, 2002).
90. Florence Buegwa, "Gender and Human Rights in Post-conflict Reconstruction," in *Women and Men in Partnership for Post-conflict Reconstruction: Report of the Sierra Leone National Consultation, Freetown, Sierra Leone 21–24 May 2001* (London: Commonwealth Secretariat, 2002), 75–81.
91. Jebbeh Forster, "HIV/AIDS: A Strategy for Sierra Leone," in *Women and Men in Partnership for Post-conflict Reconstruction: Report of the Sierra Leone National Consultation, Freetown, Sierra Leone 21–24 May 2001* (London: Commonwealth Secretariat, 2002), 143–157.
92. Ibid., 148.
93. For more details on the various roles reported by women, see chapter 3.
94. Siobhan McEvoy-Levy, ed., *Troublemakers or Peacemakers? Youth and Post-Accord Peace Building (The RIREC Project on Post-Accord Peace Building)* (Notre Dame: University of Notre Dame Press, 2006).
95. Gberie, *A Dirty War in West Africa*.
96. Edward Anague, interview by author, Freetown, Sierra Leone, December 2005.
97. Christian Aid, Sierra Leone, *What Price Peace? An Analysis f the Disarmament, Demobilization and Reintegration Plan* (London: Christian Aid, 1999).
98. Myriam Denov, "Girls in Fighting Forces: Moving beyond Victimhood" (Ottawa: CIDA, 2007), http://www.crin.org/docs/CIDA_Beyond_forces.pdf.
99. Brooks in S. Shepler, "Les filles-soldats: Trajectoires d'apres-guerre en Sierra Leone," *Politique Africaine* 88 (2002): 49–62.
100. United Nations, *From Peacekeeping to Peacebuilding: UN Strategy to Support National Recovery and Peacebuilding in Sierra Leone* (United Nations, 2002), available at http://www.reliefweb.int/library/documents/2002/undp-sle-28oct.pdf.

CHAPTER 3

1. Mohamed Sesay, interview by author, Edmonton, Alberta, October 2010.
2. Jennifer Turpin, "Many Faces: Women Confronting War," in *The Women and War Reader*, ed. Lois Lorentzen and Jennifer Turpin (New York: NYU Press, 1998), 3–19.
3. R. Charli Carpenter, *Innocent Women and Children: Gender, Norms and the Protection of Civilians* (Aldershot: Ashgate, 2006).
4. See Rawwida Baksh, Linda Etchart, Elsie Onubogu, and Tina Johnson, eds., *Gender Mainstreaming in Conflict Transformation: Building Sustainable Peace* (London: Commonwealth Secretariat, 2002).

5. Sara Ruddick, *Maternal Thinking: Towards a Politics of Peace* (Boston: Beacon Press, 1989); Mary Daly, *Pure Lust: Elemental Feminist Philosophy* (London: Women's Press, 1984).
6. April Carter, "Should Women Be Soldiers or Pacifists?" in *The Women and War Reader*, ed. Lois Lorentzen and Jennifer Turpin (New York: NYU Press, 1998), 33.
7. Patricia T. Morris, "Women, Resistance, and the Use of Force in South Africa," in *Women and the Use of Military Force*, ed. Ruth H. Howes and Michael R. Stevenson (Boulder, CO: Lynne Rienner, 1993).
8. Esther Madriz, *Nothing Bad Happens to Good Girls: Fear of Crime in Women's Lives* (Berkeley: University of California Press, 1997).
9. Ibid.
10. Merry Morash, *Understanding Gender, Crime, and Justice* (London: Sage, 2006), 137.
11. See Carpenter *Innocent Women and Children*.
12. Madriz, *Nothing Bad Happens to Good Girls*, 32.
13. Amnesty International, "Sierra Leone: Rape and Other Forms of Sexual Violence against Girls and Women," June 29, 2000, http://asiapacific.amnesty.org/library/Index/ENGAFR510352000?open&of=ENG-SLE.
14. Physicians for Human Rights, *War-Related Sexual Violence in Sierra Leone: A Population Based Assessment* (Washington, DC: Physicians for Human Rights, 2002).
15. "Gender Profile Sierra Leone," *AFROL News*, http://www.afrol.com/Categories/
16. Women/profiles/sierraleone women.htm.We the Women, "Sierra Leone's War: Women the Worst Losers," http://www.wethewomen.org/entry/help-war-time-sexual-abused-sierra-leones-woman (accessed February 21, 2005).
17. Mark Duffield, *Global Governance and the New Wars: The Merging of Development and Security* (New York: Zed Books, 2001), 123.
18. Ibid., 125.
19. World Bank, "Consultations with Youth in Sierra Leone," 2005, http://siteresources.worldbank.org/INTWDR2007/Resources/1489782-1137012196309/2112807-1150737906527/Draft_Consultations_with_youth_in_Sierra_Leone.pdf (accessed December 3, 2008).
20. Ibid. (my emphasis).
21. Tom McKinley, "Sierra Leone Diamond Town Seeks Alternative," BBC (Koidu, Sierra Leone, April 4, 2002), Africa section, http://news.bbc.co.uk/2/hi/africa/1908691.stm.
22. Women's Commission for Refugee Women and Children, "Participatory Research Study with Adolescents and Youth in Sierra Leone" (Precious Resources, 2002), www.Womenscommission.org/reports/sl/06.shtml (accessed March 30, 2006).
23. U.S. Department of State, "Country Report on Human Rights Practices 2003: Sierra Leone," Bureau of Democracy, Human Rights, and Labour, February 25,

2004, http://www.state.gov/g/drl/rls/hrrpt/2003/27750.htm (accessed April 22, 2006).
24. Interviews were conducted in confidentiality, and the names of interviewees 1 through 50 are withheld by mutual agreement. All names used in text are pseudonyms. Interviews by author, 12 November 12–December 20, 2005.
25. Interviewee 28, interview by author, Makeni, Sierra Leone, December 2005.
26. Interviewee 14, interview by author, Makeni, Sierra Leone, December 2005.
27. Interviewees 44, 12, 38, 9, 21, 22, 33, 4, 18, 39, 2, 25, 42, interview by author, Makeni, Sierra Leone, December 2005.
28. Vivi Stavrou, "Breaking the Silence: Girls Abducted during Armed Conflict in Angola," Final Report: Canadian International Development Agency and the Christian Children's Fund, Period covering September 2003–March 2005, http://www.crin.org/bcn/details.asp?id=13699&themeID=1004&topicID=1026.
29. Lene Hansen, *Security as Practice: Discourse Analysis and the Bosnian War* (London: Routledge, 2006), 99.
30. Interviewee 14, interview by author, Makeni, Sierra Leone, December 2005.
31. See chapter 2.
32. Interviewee 32, interview by author, Makeni, Sierra Leone, December 2005.
33. Interviewee 8, interview by author, Makeni, Sierra Leone, December 2005.
34. Andrea Ferrero, interview by author, Freetown, Sierra Leone, November 2005.
35. Rachel Brett, "Girl Soldiers: Challenging the Assumptions" (Quaker United Nations Office), http://www.quno.org/geneva/pdf/Girl_Soldiers.pdf.
36. Susan McKay and Dyan Mazurana, *Where Are the Girls? Girls in Fighting Forces in Northern Uganda, Sierra Leone and Mozambique: Their Lives during and after War* (Montreal: Rights and Democracy, 2004), 114.
37. Dyan Mazurana and Khristopher Carlson, *From Combat to Community: Women and Girls of Sierra Leone* (Cambridge, MA: Women Waging Peace, 2004), 21.
38. UNICEF, "The Impact of Conflict on Women and Girls in West and Central Africa and the UNICEF Response," http://www.unicef.org/publications/files/Impact_final.pdf (New York: UNICEF, 2005).
39. Glenis Taylor, interview by author, Freetown, Sierra Leone, November 2005.
40. Fr. Joseph Momoh, interview by author, Freetown, Sierra Leone, December 2005.
41. It should be noted that the intake forms for each of these children included a set list of questions for the child and a list of criteria for the social worker to fill out regarding the child. Questions included the following: Were you raped? Did you partake in drug abuse? What were you doing before the war? Criteria included information about the physical state of the child—whether the child was ill, pregnant, or disabled in any way. There was a large disparity in the amount of information included in each form. Some were complete and included additional quotations from the child, while others had questions and columns left blank. I have tried to summarize the information about these children as clearly as

possible and to present the information in a manner as close to the original forms as possible.

CHAPTER 4

1. Exceptions to this include Kathleen Staudt, Shirin M. Rai, and Jane L. Parpart, "Protesting World Trade Rules: Can We Talk about Empowerment?," *Signs* 26, no. 4 (Summer 2001): 1251–1257; Bessie House-Midamba, "The United Nations Decade: Political Empowerment or Increased Marginalization for Kenyan Women?," *Africa Today* 37, no. 1 (1990): 37–48; Jawad Syed, "Reconstructing Gender Empowerment," *Women's Studies International Forum* 33, no. 3 (2010): 283–294; and, Jane Parpart, Shirin Rai, and Kathleen Staudt, *Rethinking Empowerment: Gender and Development in a Global/Local World* (New York: Routledge, 2002).
2. Bill Cooke and Uma Kothari, eds., *Participation: The New Tyranny?* (New York: Zed Books, 2001).
3. See also Susan McKay and Dyan Mazurana, *Where Are the Girls? Girls in Fighting Forces in Northern Uganda, Sierra Leone and Mozambique: Their Lives during and after War* (Montreal: Rights and Democracy, 2004); Cynthia Cockburn, *From Where We Stand: War, Women's Activism and Feminist Analysis* (London: Zed Books, 2000); Sandra Whitworth, *Men, Militarism, and UN Peacekeeping* (Boulder, CO: Lynne Rienner, 2004).
4. Cynthia Cockburn, *The Space between Us: Negotiating Gender and National Identities in Conflict* (London: Zed Books, 1999), 7.
5. Jacqueline Stevens, *Reproducing the State* (Princeton: Princeton University Press, 1999), 22.
6. Cooke and Kothari, *Participation*; Uma Kothari, "Power, Knowledge and Social Control in Participatory Development," in *Participation: The New Tyranny?*, ed. Bill Cooke and Uma Kothari (New York: Zed Books, 2001), 139–153.
7. Kothari, "Power, Knowledge and Social Control in Participatory Development," 139–151.
8. Diana Tietjens Meyers, *Gender in the Mirror: Cultural Imagery and Women's Agency* (New York: Oxford University Press, 2002).
9. "Aid in Support of Gender Equality and Women's Empowerment: Statistics based on DAC Member's reporting on the Gender Equality Policy Maker, 2004–2005," OECD-DAC Secretariat, Creditor Reporting System database, www.oecd.org/dataoecd/7/55/38898309.pdf (accessed April 10, 2009).
10. V. Wee and N. Heyzer, *Gender, Poverty and Sustainable Development: Towards a Holistic Framework of Understanding and Action* (New York: ENGENDER, UNDP, 1996).
11. United Nations Development Fund for Women, *Resource Guide for Gender Theme Groups*, January 1, 2005, 3, http://www.unifem.org/attachments/products/ResourceGuideGenderThemeGroups_200511_eng.pdf.

12. See, for example, "A Resource Guide for Gender Theme Groups," report by the United National Development Fund for Women, New York, January 2005, http://www.undp.org.pl/files/536/resource_guide.pdf.
13. World Bank, "What Is Empowerment?," http://web.worldbank.org/WBSITE/EXTERNAL/TOPICS/EXTPOVERTY/EXTEMPOWERMENT/0,,contentMDK:20272299~menuPK:546167~pagePK:148956~piPK:216618~theSitePK:486411,00.html.
14. http://www.oecd.org/ (accessed February 22, 2009) (my emphasis).
15. Sanam Anderlini and Dyan Mazurana, "Boys and Girls Who Also Carried Guns: Forgotten in the Peace, " *New York Times*, March 12, 2004, Opinion section, http://www.nytimes.com/2004/03/12/opinion/12iht-edander_ed3_.html.
16. Dehegue Shiaka, Sulay Sesay, Edward Abu, and Joseph Momo, interviews by author, Freetown, Sierra Leone. December 2005.
17. The disarmament processes in other African countries such as the Democratic Republic of Congo and Mozambique were very similar to the model used in Sierra Leone. In these cases, the DDR was also viewed as an essential element in the transition from war to peace.
18. Mark Duffield, *Global Governance and the New Wars: The Merging of Development and Security* (New York: Zed Books, 2001).
19. Francis Kai-Kai, *National Committee for Disarmament, Demobilization and Reintegration (NCDDR) Executive Secretariat Report* (Government of Sierra Leone, 2004), 1.
20. National Committee for Disarmament, Demobilization and Reintegration, *The DDR Program: Status and Strategies for Completion* (Freetown, Sierra Leone: Government of Sierra Leone, 2002), http://siteresources.worldbank.org/SIERRALEONEEXTN/ Resources/ddr_status.pdf.
21. Adekeye Adebajo and David Keen, "Sierra Leone," in *United Nations Interventionism 1991–2004*, ed. Mats Berdal and Spyros Economides (New York: Cambridge University Press, 1996), 246–247.
22. Ibid.
23. National Committee for Disarmament, Demobilization and Reintegration, *The DDR Program*, 7.
24. Ibid., 18.
25. Ibid.
26. Ibid., 8.
27. Ibid., 5.
28. United Nations Disarmament, Demobilization and Reintegration Resource Center, *National Institutions for DDR* (United Nations), http://www.unddr.org/iddrs/03/30.php.
29. Tobias Pietz, "Gaps and Trends in Disarmament, Demobilization, and Reintegration Programs of the United Nations," in *Small Arms—Big Problem: A Global Threat to Peace, Security and Development* (Vienna: Schriftenreihe der Landesverteidigungsakademie, 2007), 62.

30. Kai-Kai, *National Committee for Disarmament Demobilization and Reintegration (NCDDR) Executive Secretariat Report*.
31. *USAID's Strategy in Sierra Leone* (USAID, 2007), http:// www.usaid.gov/locations/sub-saharan_africa/countries/sierraleone/.
32. Ibid.
33. Ibid.
34. Ibid.
35. Child Protection Committees of Sierra Leone, "Position Paper on Psychosocial Interventions for Children in Need of Special Protection" (Freetown, Sierra Leone, March 1998), http://www.essex.ac.uk/armedcon/story_id/000016.htm, p. 4 (my emphasis).
36. Ibid., 4–6.
37. "Sierra Leone," *Escola de Cultura de Pau*, 2006, http://escolapau.uab.cat/img/programas/desarme/mapa/sierrai.pdf.
38. United Nations, *UN Strategy to Support National Recovery and Peacebuilding in Sierra Leone* (United Nations, 2002), http://www.reliefweb.int/library/documents/2002/undp-sle-28oct.pdf, p. 21 (my emphasis).
39. See also S. Shepler, "Les filles-soldats: Trajectoires d'apres-guerre en Sierra Leone," *Politique Africaine* 88 (2002): 49–62.
40. Bintue J. Magona, Sulay Sesay, Hamidu Jalloh, interviews by author, Freetown, Sierra Leone, November and December 2005.
41. Executive Secretariat Information and Sensitization Unit, *Information Bulletin* (Freetown, Sierra Leone: World Bank, 2000), http://www.worldbank.org/ afr/ afth2/crrp/bulletin9-8.html.
42. Ibid.
43. Shepler, "Les filles-soldats"; Guilia Baldi and Megan MacKenzie, "Silent Identities: Children Born of War in Sierra Leone," in *Born of War: Protecting Children of Sexual Violence Survivors in Conflict Zones*, ed. R. Charli Carpenter (Bloomfield, CT: Kumarian Press, 2007), 78–94.
44. Interviewee 42, interview by author, Makeni, Sierra Leone, ecember 16, 2005.
45. Shepler, "Les filles-soldats."
46. Stevens, *Reproducing the State*, 22.
47. Lene Hansen, *Security as Practice: Discourse Analysis and the Bosnian War* (London: Routledge, 2006), 21.
48. Sulay Sesay, interview by author, Freetown, Sierra Leone, December 2005.
49. Edward Anague, interview by author, Freetown, Sierra Leone, December 2005.
50. Isha Kamara, interview by author, Makeni, Sierra Leone, November 2005.
51. Fr. Joseph Momoh, interview by author, Makeni, Sierra Leone, December 2005.
52. Interviewee 67, interview by author, Makeni, Sierra Leone, December 2005.
53. Interviewee 73, interview by author, Makeni, Sierra Leone, December 2005.
54. Interviewee 59, interview by author, Makeni, Sierra Leone, December 2005.

55. Interviewees 70, 62, 54, interview by author, Makeni, Sierra Leone, December 2005.
56. Interviewees 58, 57, interview by author, Makeni, Sierra Leone, December 2005.
57. Interviewee 68, interview by author, Makeni, Sierra Leone, December 2005.
58. Interviewee 56, interview by author, Makeni, Sierra Leone, December 2005.
59. Interviewee 42, interview by author, Makeni, Sierra Leone, December 2005.
60. Interviewee 11, interview by author, Makeni, Sierra Leone, December 2005.
61. Interviewees 11, 22, 24, 53, 67, interview by author, Makeni, Sierra Leone, December 2005.
62. Interviewee 5, interview by author, Makeni, Sierra Leone, December 2005.
63. Interviewee 37, interview by author, Makeni, Sierra Leone, December 2005.
64. Interviewee 18, interview by author, Makeni, Sierra Leone, December 2005.
65. Executive Secretariat Information and Sensitization Unit, *Information Bulletin*.

CHAPTER 5

1. Edward Anague, interview by author, Freetown, Sierra Leone, December 2005.
2. This amount was paid to ex-combatants as a start-up grant during the first phase; it was not given to all combatants as funding ran out and training opportunities began to be suggested.
3. Lene Hansen, *Security as Practice: Discourse Analysis and the Bosnian War* (London: Routledge, 2006). p31
4. See "The World Bank, Sierra Leone: Disarmament, Demobilization and Reintegration (DDR) in 'The World Bank's Engagement Africa Region,'" Good Practice Infobrief, World Bank, no. 81, October 2002, http://www.worldbank.org/afr/findings/infobeng/infob81.pdf.
5. These estimates were confirmed by Sulay Sesay (Information and Sensitization Unit manager, DDR/project manager, Capacity Development in Sierra Leone). Sulay Sesay, interview by author, Freetown, Sierra Leone, December 16, 2005. See also Sanam Anderlini and Dyan Mazurana, "Boys and Girls Who Also Carried Guns: Forgotten in the Peace," *International Herald Tribune* op-ed, March 12, 2004.
6. Dyan Mazurana and Khristopher Carlson, *From Combat to Community: Women and Girls of Sierra Leone* (Cambridge, MA: Women Waging Peace, 2004).
7. "The Impact of Conflict on Women and Girls in West and Central Africa and the UNICEF Response," UNICEF, February 2005, http://www.unicef.org/publications/files/Impact final.pdf.
8. Ibid.
9. Ibid.
10. Ibid.
11. Interviewee 23, interview by author, Freetown, Sierra Leone, December 2005.
12. Interviewee 17, interview by author, Freetown, Sierra Leone, December 2005.

13. Interviewee 49, interview by author, Freetown, Sierra Leone, December 2005.
14. Interviewee 1, interview by author, Freetown, Sierra Leone, December 2005.
15. Talking Drum Studio was a multimedia studio established to encourage dialogue and exchange related to national issues.
16. Interviewee 25, interview by author, Freetown, Sierra Leone, December 2005.
17. Interviewee 1, interview by author, Freetown, Sierra Leone, December 2005.
18. Interviewee 18, interview by author, Freetown, Sierra Leone, December 2005.
19. Interviewee 42, interview by author, Freetown, Sierra Leone, December 2005.
20. Interviewee 44, interview by author, Freetown, Sierra Leone, December 2005.
21. Interviewee 37, interview by author, Freetown, Sierra Leone, December 2005.
22. Interviewee 12, interview by author, Freetown, Sierra Leone, December 2005.
23. Interviewee 8, interview by author, Freetown, Sierra Leone, December 2005.
24. Interviewee 19, interview by author, Freetown, Sierra Leone, December 2005.
25. Interviewee 25, interview by author, Freetown, Sierra Leone, December 2005.
26. Interviewee 42, interview by author, Freetown, Sierra Leone, December 2005.
27. Interviewee 23, interview by author, Freetown, Sierra Leone, December 2005.
28. Interviewee 43, interview by author, Freetown, Sierra Leone, December 2005.
29. Interviewee 42, interview by author, Freetown, Sierra Leone, December 2005.
30. Interviewees 19, 42, 43, 26, interview by author, Freetown, Sierra Leone, December 2005.

CHAPTER 6

1. Edward Anague, interview by author, Freetown, Sierra Leone, December 2005.
2. Jacqueline Stevens, *Reproducing the State* (Princeton: Princeton University Press, 1999).
3. Ibid., 210.
4. Susan Brownmiller, *Against Our Will: Men, Women and Rape* (New York: Simon and Schuster, 1975).
5. T. Meron, "Rape as a Crime under International Humanitarian Law," *American Journal of International Law* 87, no. 3 (1993): 424–428; Joanne Barkan, "As Old as War Itself: Rape in Foca," *Dissent* 49, no. 1 (Winter 2002): 60–67; Karen Engle, "Feminism and Its (Dis)contents: Criminalizing Wartime Rape in Bosnia and Herzegovina," *American Journal of International Law* 99, no. 4 (2005): 778–816.
6. M. A Tétreault, "Justice for All: Wartime Rape and Women's Human Rights," *Global Governance* 3 (1997): 197–212; A Barstow, "Introduction," in *War's Dirty Secret: Rape, Prostitution, and Other Crimes against Women*, ed. Anne Llewellyn Barstow (Cleveland, OH: Pilgrim Press, 2000), 1–12; Miranda Alison, "Wartime Sexual Violence: Women's Human Rights and Questions of Masculinity," *Review of International Studies* 33, no. 1 (2007): 75–90.
7. L. Hansen, "Gender, Nation, Rape: Bosnia and the Construction of Security," *International Feminist Journal of Politics* 3, no. 1 (2000): 55–75; C. S. Snyder et al.,

"On the Battleground of Women's Bodies: Mass Rape in Bosnia-Herzegovina," *Affilia* 21, no. 2 (2006): 184–195.
8. Maria B. Olujic, "Embodiment of Terror: Gendered Violence in Peacetime and Wartime in Croatia and Bosnia-Herzegovina," *Medical Anthropology Quarterly*, n.s., 12, no. 1 (1998): 31–50; Helen Liebling-Kalifani et al., "Violence against Women in Northern Uganda: The Neglected Health Consequences of War," *Journal of International Women's Studies* 9, no. 3 (2008): 179–190.
9. Alexandra Stiglmayer, "The Rapes in Bosnia-Herzegovina," in *Mass Rape: The War against Women in Bosnia-Herzegovina*, ed. Alexandra Stiglmayer, trans. Marion Faber (Lincoln: University of Nebraska Press, 1994), 54–72.
10. Cynthia Enloe, *Globalization and Militarism: Feminists Make the Link* (Plymouth, UK: Rowman and Littlefield, 2007).
11. L. Kelly, "Wars against Women: Sexual Violence, Sexual Politics and the Militarised State," in *States of Conflict: Gender, Violence and Resistance*, ed. Susie Jacobs, Ruth Jacobson, and Jennifer Marchbank (London: Zed Books, 2000), 45–65.
12. Jan Jindy Pettman, *Worlding Women: A Feminist International Politics* (London: Routledge, 1996).
13. Claudia Card, "Rape as a Weapon of War," *Hypatia* 11, no. 4 (1996): 5–18.
14. Nancy Farwell, "War Rape: New Conceptualizations and Responses," *Affilia* 19, no. 4 (2004): 389–403.
15. See Beverly Allen, *Rape Warfare: The Hidden Genocide in Bosnia-Herzegovina and Croatia* (Minneapolis: University of Minnesota Press, 1996); S. Kamal, "The 1971 Genocide in Bangladesh and Crimes Committed against Women," in *Common Grounds: Sexual Violence against Women in War and Armed Conflict Situations*, ed. Indai Lourdes Sajor (Tokyo: Asian Center for Women's Human Rights, 1998), 268–281; Marion Pratt and Leah Werchick, *Sexual Terrorism: Rape as a Weapon of War in Eastern Democratic Republic of Congo: An Assessment of Programmatic Responses to Sexual Violence in North Kivu, South Kivu, Maniema, and Orientale* (Washington, DC: USAID/DCHA, 2004); E. J. Wood, "Armed Groups and Sexual Violence: When Is Wartime Rape Rare?," *Politics and Society* 37, no. 1 (2009): 131–161.
16. C. Kennedy-Pipe and P. Stanley, "Rape in War: Lessons of the Balkan Conflict in the 1990s," *International Journal of Human Rights* 3, no. 4 (2000): 67–84.
17. Stiglmayer, "The Rapes in Bosnia-Herzegovina"; R. Coomaraswamy, *Report of the Special Rapporteur on Violence against Women, Its Causes and Consequences* (Geneva: United Nations, 1998); Olujic, "Embodiment of Terror."
18. Farwell, "War Rape," 395.
19. Card, "Rape as a Weapon of War"; Coomaraswamy, *Report of the Special Rapporteur on Violence against Women*; Olujic, "Embodiment of Terror."
20. Sharon Frederick, *Rape: Weapon of Terror* (River Edge, NJ: World Scientific, 2001), 19.
21. Pratt and Werchick, *Sexual Terrorism*, 8.

22. UNICEF, "The State of the World's Children: Sexual Violence as a Weapon of War," 1996, http://www.unicef.org/sowc96pk/sexviol.htm, p. 1 (accessed January 12, 2008).
23. Frederick, *Rape*, 14.
24. Julie A. Mertus, *War's Offensive on Women: The Humanitarian Challenge in Bosnia, Kosovo, and Afghanistan* (San Francisco: Kumarian Press, 2000), 77 (my emphasis).
25. Stevens, *Reproducing the State*, 108.
26. A rope is tied around a kola fruit, and the two parties pull either side of the rope to break the kola.
27. Valerie Nicol, "Promoting Gender Equality through Legal Reform," in *Women and Men in Partnership for Post-conflict Reconstruction: Report of the Sierra Leone National Consultation, Freetown, Sierra Leone, 21–24 May 2001* (London: Commonwealth Secretariat, 2002), 72.
28. Ibid., 71.
29. Barbara E. Harrell-Bond and Ulrica Rijnsdorp, *Family Law in Sierra Leone* (Leiden: Afrika-Studiecentrum, 1975), 27.
30. Nicol, "Promoting Gender Equality through Legal Reform."
31. Harrell-Bond and Rijnsdorp, *Family Law in Sierra Leone*.
32. The Sierra Leone Truth and Reconciliation Commission (TRC), "Witness to Truth: Report of the Sierra Leone Truth and Reconciliation Commission," 2004, http://www.trcsierraleone.org/drwebsite/publish/index.shtm.
33. Florence Buegwa, "Gender and Human Rights in Post-conflict Reconstruction," in *Women and Men in Partnership for Post-conflict Reconstruction: Report of the Sierra Leone National Consultation* (London: Commonwealth Secretariat, 2002), 84.
34. Jebbeh Forster, "HIV/AIDS: A Strategy for Sierra Leone," in *Women and Men in Partnership for Post-conflict Reconstruction: Report of the Sierra Leone National Consultation* (London: Commonwealth Secretariat, 2002), 148.
35. Ibid.
36. Physicians for Human Rights, *War-Related Sexual Violence in Sierra Leone: A Population Based Assessment* (Washington, DC: Physicians for Human Rights, 2002).
37. Amnesty International, "Sierra Leone: Rape and Other Forms of Sexual Violence against Girls and Women," June 29, 2000, http://asiapacific.amnesty.org/library/Index/ENGAFR510352000?open&of=ENG-SLE (accessed November 8, 2006).
38. Physicians for Human Rights, *War-Related Sexual Violence in Sierra Leone*; Megan MacKenzie, "The International Politics of Rape, Sex and the Family in Sierra Leone," Institute for Security Studies, ISS Paper 203 (October 2009).
39. Megan MacKenzie, "Securitizing Sex? Towards a Theory of the Utility of Wartime Sexual Violence," *International Feminist Journal of Politics* 12, no. 2 (2010): 202.
40. Physicians for Human Rights, *War-Related Sexual Violence in Sierra Leone*.

41. Susan McKay and Dyan Mazurana, *Where Are the Girls? Girls in Fighting Forces in Uganda, Sierra Leone and Mozambique: Their Lives during and after the War* (Montreal: Rights and Democracy, 2004).
42. It is notable that the term "bush wife" is often used interchangeably with "sex slave." Rather than using terms like "rape" and "gang rape," a woman typically would say that a man took her as his wife.
43. Human Rights Watch, *Sexual Violence within the Sierra Leone Conflict*, February 23, 2001, http://www.hrw.org (accessed February 2, 2005).
44. Physicians for Human Rights, *War-Related Sexual Violence in Sierra Leone: A Population Based Assessment* (Washington, DC: Physicians for Human Rights, January 2002).
45. Forster, "HIV/AIDS," 149.
46. MacKenzie, "Securitizing Sex?"
47. Physicians for Human Rights, *War-Related Sexual Violence in Sierra Leone.*
48. Joe Pemagbi, "The Challenge to Democracy in Sierra Leone," in *Women and Men in Partnership for Post-conflict Reconstruction: Report of the Sierra Leone National Consultation, Freetown, Sierra Leone 21–24 May 2001* (London: Commonwealth Secretariat, 2002), 27–38.
49. Hamidu Jalloh, interview by author, Freetown, Sierra Leone, December 2005.
50. Ibid.
51. Physicians for Human Rights, *War-Related Sexual Violence in Sierra Leone.*
52. Ibid.
53. Radio Netherlands Worldwide, "War Rape and Sexual Assault," 2000, http://www.radionetherlands.nl/features/humanrights/rape.html (accessed January 28, 2007).
54. Sulay Sesay, interview by author, Freetown, Sierra Leone, December 2005.
55. Guilia Baldi and Megan MacKenzie, "Silent Identities: Children Born of War in Sierra Leone," in *Born of War: Protecting Children of Sexual Violence Survivors in Conflict Zones*, ed. R. Charli Carpenter (Bloomfield, CT: Kumarian Press, 2007), 78–94.
56. Interviewee 13, interview by author, Freetown, Sierra Leone, December 2005.
57. S. Shepler, "Les filles-soldats: Trajectoires d'apres-guerre en Sierra Leone," *Politique Africaine* 88 (2002): 49–62.
58. Ibid., 58.
59. Lene Hansen, "The Little Mermaid's Silent Security Dilemma and the Absence of Gender in the Copenhagen School," *Millennium: Journal of International Studies* 29, no. 2 (2000): 285–306.
60. Sierra Leone Office of the Attorney General and Ministry of Justice Special Court Task Force, "Statute for the Special Court of Sierra Leone," 2002.
61. A complete record of the trial and the judgment can be found at http://www.sc-sl.org/CASES/ArmedForcesRevolutionaryCouncilAFRCComplete/AFRCJudgment/tabid/173/Default.aspx.

62. K Glassborow, "Forced Marriage Appeal May Influence ICC," 2007, http://www.wluml.org/node/3907 (accessed February 8, 2008).
63. Ibid.
64. Special Court for Sierra Leone, "Decision on Prosecution Request for Leave to Amend the Indictment. Office of the Prosecutor, 6 May," Freetown, Sierra Leone, 2004, http://www.sc-sl.org/CASES/ProsecutorvsFofanaandKondewaCDFCase/TrialChamberDecisions/tabid/153/Default.aspx. (accessed December 23 2011).
65. Quoted in Glassborow, "Forced Marriage Appeal May Influence ICC."
66. M. Scharf and S. Mattler, "Forced Marriage: Exploring the Viability of the Special Court for Sierra Leone's New Crime against Humanity," Case Research Papers Series in Legal Studies, 2005, Working Paper 05-35, p. 15.
67. J. Morley, "Forced Marriage Is a Crime against Humanity," 2008, http://www.internationalfamilylawfirm.com/2008/10/forced-marriage-is-crime-against.html (accessed December 2, 2008).
68. Ibid.

CHAPTER 7

1. Interviewee 11, interview by author, Freetown, Sierra Leone, December 2005.
2. Interviewee 61, interview by author, Freetown, Sierra Leone, December 2005.
3. Sara Ruddick, *Maternal Thinking: Towards a Politics of Peace* (Boston: Beacon Press, 1989).
4. In L. Kelly, "Wars against Women: Sexual Violence, Sexual Politics and the Militarised State," in *States of Conflict: Gender, Violence and Resistance*, ed. Susie Jacobs, Ruth Jacobson, and Jennifer Marchbank (London: Zed Books, 2000), 52.
5. Jacques Donzelot, *The Policing of Families* (London: Hutchinson, 1979); Jacqueline Stevens, *Reproducing the State* (Princeton: Princeton University Press, 1999).
6. Lene Hansen, *Security as Practice: Discourse Analysis and the Bosnian War* (London: Routledge, 2006), 19.
7. Barbara E. Harrell-Bond and Ulrica Rijnsdorp, *Family Law in Sierra Leone* (Leiden: Afrika-Studiecentrum, 1975), 44.
8. The definitions of "child" and "adult" vary between ethnic groups and from region to region in Sierra Leone. For example, a former British act called the Young People's Act identified anyone over age sixteen as an adult; another law designates fourteen as the threshold between childhood and adulthood. Traditionally, in some chiefdoms both male and female children go through initiation ceremonies, which can include female genital mutilation, training in local hunting procedures, and learning about the history of the tribe. These ceremonies dictate the transition from childhood to adulthood but can be performed at a variety of ages depending on the physical development of the child and the financial resources of the family.
9. Dehunge Shiaka, interview by author, Freetown, Sierra Leone, December 2005.
10. Ibid.
11. Dehunge Shiaka, interview by author, Edmonton, Alberta, November 2007.

12. Ibid.
13. Barbara E. Harrell-Bond and Ulrica Rijnosdorp, *Family Law in Sierra Leone: A Research Report* (Leiden: Afrika-Studiecentrum, 1975), 20.
14. This mirrors British common law.
15. Harrell-Bond and Rijnosdorp, *Family Law in Sierra Leone*, 45.
16. Ibid., 45–49.
17. A caretaker marriage or union consists of a woman estranged or separated from her husband who becomes involved in a conjugal union. It is described as a "caretaker" marriage because the male partner assumes the role of caretaker in place of the previous husband.
18. A debtor-creditor marriage comes about when a woman wishes to divorce her husband but is unable to pay back the initial dowry. The husband can suggest that the woman obtain the money by finding a wealthy man and pledging her services until the debt is paid.
19. Dehunge Shiaka, interview by author, Freetown, Sierra Leone, December 2005.
20. Ibid.
21. Interviewees 49, 12, 37, 22, interview by author, Freetown, Sierra Leone, December 2005.
22. Mameh Kargbo, Cooperazeone Internazionale (COOPI), interview by author, Freetown, Sierra Leone, November 30, 2005.
23. Interviewee 33, interview by author, Freetown, Sierra Leone, December 2005.
24. Mameh Kargbo, Cooperazeone Internazionale (COOPI), interview by author, Freetown, Sierra Leone, November 30, 2005.
25. Dehunge Shiaka, Ministry of Social Welfare, Gender and Children's Affairs Sierra Leone, interview by author, Freetown, Sierra Leone, 15 December 2005.
26. Glenis Taylor, UNICEF, interview by author, Freetown, Sierra Leone. December 2, 2005.
27. Augustan Turai, Ben Hirsh Society, interview by author, Freetown, Sierra Leone, November 11, 2005.
28. The CIS is one of the first organizations to address the needs of abandoned children during the conflict; interview by author, Freetown, Sierra Leone, December 1, 2005.
29. Ibid.
30. Giulia Baldi and Megan MacKenzie, "Silent Identities: Children Born of War in Sierra Leone," in *Born of War: Protecting Children of Sexual Violence survivors*, ed. R. Charli Carpenter (Bloomfield, CT: Kumarian Press, 2007).
31. Augustan Turai, interview by author, Freetown, Sierra Leone, December 2005.
32. Rev. Hassan Mansaray, interview by author, Freetown, Sierra Leone, December 2005.
33. "Banfa baby" is a term used to describe a baby who falls ill when still breast-feeding. The connotation attached to this term is that there is something wrong with the woman and that she has potentially had an affair on her husband.

34. Francis Lahai, interview by author, Freetown, Sierra Leone, December 2005.
35. Rev. Hassan Mansaray, interview by author, Freetown, Sierra Leone, December 2005.
36. Baldi and MacKenzie, "Silent Identities," 90.
37. Ibid., 91.
38. Stevens, *Reproducing the State*, 223.
39. Francis Lahai, Street Children's Task Force, interview by author, Freetown, Sierra Leone, November 30, 2005.
40. Ibid.
41. Augustan Binue, Ben Hirsh Society, interview by author, November 11, 2005.
42. Dehunge Shiaka, MSWGCA, interview by author, Freetown, Sierra Leone, December 15, 2005.
43. Glenis Taylor, interview by author, Freetown, Sierra Leone, December 2005.
44. Ibid.
45. Hansen, *Security as Practice*, 35.

CHAPTER 8

1. Cassandra Clifford, "War's Sexual Violence towards Girls," August 2, 2007, http://children.foreignpolicyblogs.com/2007/08/02/wars-sexual-violence-towards-girls/ (accessed December 10, 2010); see also IRIN, "In Depth: Broken Bodies, Broken Dreams: Violence against Women Exposed," http://www.irinnews.org/IndepthMain.aspx?IndepthId=59&ReportId=72831.
2. http://www.un.org/ecosocdev/geninfo/afrec/vol18no4/184sierraleone.htm.
3. http://www.unisa.edu.au/hawkecentre/events/2008events/RedCross.asp.
4. http://warcrimes.foreignpolicyblogs.com/2008/01/09/and-more-charles-taylor/.
5. Hamidu Jalloh, interview by author, Freetown, Sierra Leone, December 2005.
6. Edward Anague, interview by author, Freetown, Sierra Leone, December 2005.
7. Interviewee 8, interview by author, Makeni, Sierra Leone, December 2005.

INDEX

Abrahamsen, Rita, 7, 148n22
Adoption. *See* Family
Africa, 26; representations of, 1–2, 23, 28, 30, 137; women soldiers and, 9, 48
AFROL, 49, 156n16
Amnesty International, 49, 156n13, 164n37
Amputation, 34–35, 54–57, 63, 138
Armed Forces Revolutionary Council, 18, 31–32, 34, 41, 52, 54, 56, 59, 85, 89, 95, 112–114, 165n62
Augustan Bintue Ogranization, 72, 123, 129–130, 133, 154n82

Bastardy Act. *See* Family
Ben Hirsh Society, 129, 133, 167n27, 168n41
Blood diamonds, 23, 151n3
Brett, Rachel, 56, 149n29, 149n31, 157n38
British Broadcasting Corporation (BBC), 33, 147n1, 156n24
British troops, 32, 36–37
Brownmiller, Susan, 101, 162n4
Burton, Richard, 28, 152n34
Butler, Josephine, 27, 150n54

Carlson, Kristopher, 56, 149n31, 157n40, 161n6
Carpenter, Charli, 9, 148n24, 150n51, 155n3, 156n11, 160n43, 165n56, 167n30
Child Protection Committees of Sierra Leone, 71, 160n35
Children Associated with the War (CAW), 45, 55, 57–60, 74, 129, 150n59, 154n82
Children Integrated Services (CIS), 75, 79, 123–124, 131, 167n28
Child soldiers, 1, 23, 57, 140, 147n14, 151n5; and the DDR process, 55, 71, 78–79; definitions of, 20–21, 119, 134; girl soldiers, 41, 58–61, 107, 149n29; unaccompanied children distinction. 58. *See also* Ex-combatants
Civil Defence Forces, 18, 31, 37–38, 41, 68, 70, 94, 96, 108, 112, 166n65. *See also* Kamajors
Colonial era: and British law, 17, 29–30, 104–105; legacy, 25–27, 30, 145. *See also* Marriage; Prostitution
Community Extension Development Association (CEDA), 41, 75, 93, 150n59
Conciliation Resources, 41
Conjugal order, 113–116, 119–122, 132, 141–142; definition of, 3–5, 45–46; disruption of, 16, 51, 100–101, 109, 113; neoliberal interpretations of, 15, 64–65, 135; in Sierra Leone, 17, 27, 42, 74, 104, 106; as a theoretical tool, 10–14
Contagious disease laws, 28
Convention on the Rights of the Child, 79
Cooke, Bill, 65, 158n2, 158n6

>> 169

Cooperazeone Internazionale (COOPI), 77, 150n59, 167n22, 167n24
Copenhagen School, 7–8, 62, 67, 110, 165n60. *See also* Hansen, Lene
Creoles, 25–26. *See also* Sexual slavery
Crimes against humanity, 112–114
Custody laws. *See* Family
Customary law, 29–30, 105–106, 120–122
Customary unions, 29, 105

Dalla Costa, Mariarosa, 27, 152n27
Deleuze, Gilles, 12, 149n45
Democratic Republic of the Congo, 46, 103, 115, 147n5, 159n17, 163n15
Denov, Myriam, 9, 41, 148n26, 149n28, 151n5, 155n98
Development: gendered nature of, 14, 64–84; liberal project of, 64–84, 138, 142, 145; policy, 46, 63, 66, 118, 142–143; prevailing assumptions, 5–8; securitization of, 61, 133–134, 143, 147n1; social and moral objectives of, 12
Diamonds. *See* Natural resources
Disarmament, Demobilization and Reintegration (DDR): empowerment and, 68–72, 80–84; failures, 38–40, 43, 69–78, 85–97; fear of attending, 91–93, 96; funding of, 38; process, 14, 18, 31, 37–39, 55–57, 139, 142–143 147n5, 159n17, 161n4; requirement to surrender a weapon, 88–89; Sierra Leonean critiques of, 74–79; stigma associated with, 90–92
Discourse analysis, 9–10, 15, 17, 28, 62–66, 71, 83, 85–86, 115, 145
Donzelot, Jacques, 10–13, 149n41, 166n4
Duffield, Mark, 50, 68, 147n6, 147n7, 156n20, 159n18

Economic Community of West African States Monitoring Group (ECOMOG), 32, 34–35, 59, 124–125
Enloe, Cynthia, 9, 65, 102, 163n10
Empowerment: disarmament demobilization reintegration and, 64, 69–74, 86; female soldiers and, 80–83; as a naturalization process, 73–74, 80–82; neoliberalism and, 15, 67, 159n13; through war activities, 83; women's empowerment, 21, 63–64, 66–67, 158n1; and youth, 70
Ex-combatants, 6, 37–38, 68–70, 74, 150n63, 154n77, 161n2; children and youths, 38, 57, 72–73; disabled, 38, 73; female, 38, 72–73, 76, 85, 88–92, 95, 143; male, 73, 83. *See also* Female soldiers
Executive Outcomes (EO), 32, 34, 94

Family, 4, 10–13, 38; Bastardy Act, 121; custody in Sierra Leone, 120–122; Foucault and, 11–12; liberal model of, 15–16, 27, 29, 82–83, 119, 132; (re)construction of, 51, 58, 65, 73, 115, 119–120, 142; Sierra Leone context, 100, 104–109, 131; and wartime rape, 55, 100–111, 115, 141, 164n39. *See also* Marriage
Family law, 17, 25, 29–30, 101, 115, 121, 153n39
Family planning, 14
Female circumcision, 25, 29, 79
Female-headed households, 14
Female soldiers, 1–2; combatant distinction, 42, 52–54; as a conjugal order problem, 4, 17; define themselves, 51–56; disarmament demobilization reintegration and, 38, 42, 64, 72–97, 137–139, 143; empowerment, 41, 80–84; interviews with, 2–3, 16, 18, 20–21, 87–88, 125; mainstream narratives, 2, 137;

number of, in Sierra Leone, 39, 41, 51, 54; renaming of, 15, 46–62, 144; representations of, 6, 46–48, 66; in support roles, 52–53
Feminism: on gender and war, 8–10, 145–146, 148n24, 148n26, 156n5, 158n3; methodology, 17; theory, 21, 64–66, 101, 115, 118–119
Forum for African Women Educationalists (FAWE) Rape Victims Programme, 40, 106
Foucault, Michel, 10–13, 65, 149n36
Fouray Bay College, 26
Freetown, 17, 19, 26, 32–35, 40, 60, 78, 92, 104–106, 109–110, 139–140, 142–143, 153n53

Gberie, Lansana, 27, 31, 35, 151n3
Gender: binaries, 45, 51; hierarchies, 58, 65, 74, 100–101, 112; identities, 7, 13–14, 21, 46, 86; order, 3–5, 10–12, 15, 17, 23–26, 64–66, 113, 115, 134, 138, 141, 146; representations of war, 2–3, 8–9, 22, 62, 87, 145, 148n24, 148n26; roles, 9, 73, 40, 48–49, 52–53, 61, 72–73, 82–83
Guinea, 23, 33, 94

Hansen, Lene, 11, 13, 17, 46, 65, 74, 85, 119, 133, 148n23, 150n52, 157n32, 160n47, 161n3, 162n7, 165n60, 166n6, 168n45
Human Rights Watch, 108, 150n59, 165n44

Idle: men, 2, 14, 50–51; women and girls, 51; World Bank definition of, 50; youth, 50
International aid agencies, 62
International Mission and Training (IMAT), 32
International non-governmental organizations (INGO), 1, 86; staff, 140
Ivory Coast, 34, 94–95

Kabbah, Ahmad Tejan, 34, 37, 151n3
Kai-Kai, Francis, 39, 70, 159n19, 160n30
Kamajors, 18, 31, 54, 93. *See also* Civil Defence Forces
Kaplan, Robert, 30, 150n2, 153n43
Koroma, Major John Paul, 34
Kothari, Uma, 15, 65–66, 158n2, 158n6, 158n7

Lazar, Michelle, 17, 150n54, 150n55
Liberia, 23, 30, 33, 60, 147n5
Libya, 31
Lome Peace Accord, 35–36, 37, 40, 68

MacKenzie, Megan, 160n43, 164n39, 164n40, 165n47, 165n56, 167n30, 168n36
Manderson, Lenore, 27, 152n26
Marriage, 104–106; forced, 112–115, 144, 166n63, 166n66; gender subordination and, 12, 100–101; regulation of, 4, 10, 13, 42, 119, 126, 134, 141; in Sierra Leone, 29–30, 104–106, 167n17, 150n58; war, 22, 73, 102–103, 111. *See also* Family
Masculinity, 15, 58, 62, 65, 101–102, 115–116, 145, 162n6
Mazurana, Dyan, 7, 56, 108, 148n16, 149n31, 150n62, 157n39, 157n40, 158n3 159n15, 161n5, 161n6, 165n42
McKay, Susan, 7, 56, 108, 148n16, 148n17, 148n19, 149n31, 150n62, 157n39, 158n3, 165n42
Medicins Sans Frontieres, 110
Methodology, 17–22
Microcredit programs, 38, 73, 82–83
Millennium Development Goals (MDGs), 67

Militarization and militarized societies, 102
Ministry of Social Welfare, Gender and Children's Affairs (MSWGCA), 107, 120–121, 128, 130, 132, 167n25, 168n42
Momoh, Father Joseph, 24–25, 33, 78–79, 151n9, 151n11, 157n43, 160n51

National Committee for Disarmament Demobilization and Reintegration (NCDDR), 7, 37–39, 57, 69–73, 79, 148n15, 154n85, 159n19
National Provisional Ruling Council, 32–33
Natural resources, 26; diamonds, 23, 31, 127, 151n3; Natural Resources Commission, 35
New humanitarianism, 12, 149n44
Nigeria, 34; role in ECOMOG, 32
Non-governmental organization (NGO), 1–6, 41, 48; and the DDR, 92; and empowerment, 15, 64, 76; role in Sierra Leone, 61, 132–134; staff, 47, 101, 140; policy, 18, 50, 86, 143;
Nuclear family. *See* Family

Operation No Living Thing, 19, 35
Organization for Economic Cooperation and Development (OECD), 64, 67, 149n30, 158n9, 159n14
Orphans, 14, 134

Parashar, Swati, 9, 148n26, 148n27
Paternity, 4, 12, 30, 100, 120–122, 125–127, 135. *See also* Family
Patriarchy, 17, 145; patriarchal norms, 3, 100–103, 115; relations in war, 7, 102
Peacebuilding, 42, 155n100
Peacekeepers, 36, 118, 124–125, 132, 140
Philanthropy, 10–12
Phillips, Richard, 27, 152n17

Physicians for Human Rights, 40, 49, 106, 108, 110, 155n89, 164n39
Polygamy, 29
Postcolonial, 9–10, 27, 42, 64, 141, 145, 152n17
Post-conflict: definitions of, 144; development policies in Sierra Leone, 5, 14, 18, 65, 74–75, 119; as gendered, 3–9, 42, 46, 61–62, 155n90; idealized imaginary of, 2, 137–141; mainstream accounts of, 3; narratives, 15, 21–22, 70; policies, 46, 50–53, 65, 86, 110, 134; politics, 47
Post-Conflict Reintegration Initiative for Development and Empowerment (PRIDE), 20, 150n63
Prostitution, 51, 76, 112, 124–125, 162n6; during the colonial period in Sierra Leone 27–28

Radicalization of development: gender and, 14, 133; post-conflict development and, 144, 147n6; securing and, 5–8, 61, 68
Rape: children born as a result, 4, 22, 73, 101, 109, 118–119, 124–130, 144, 150n51; feminist scholarship and, 101–103; impacts of, 109–110; during the Sierra Leone conflict, 49, 55, 58–60, 106–108, 118, 156n13; role of NGOs post-conflict, 132–134; stigma of, 109–112, 119–123, 130–132; as a tool of war, 16, 40, 99–116, 141, 144
Reconstruction: as gendered, 3, 22, 47, 62, 65, 97, 144, 148n25, 155n90, 155n91, 164n27; policies, 3–8, 68
Rehabilitation, 6–7; policies in Sierra Leone, 68, 132; as gendered, 3, 8, 138, 144
Reintegration: failures in Sierra Leone, 74–83, 89, 138–139, 142; as gendered, 3, 14–18, 42, 97, 144; process in

Sierra Leone, 39, 64–74, 87, 132; root of concept, 6–7, 68. *See also* Disarmament, Demobilization and Reintegration

Return to normal, 6; as gendered, 1, 3, 74, 82, 135

Revolutionary United Front, 18, 31–41, 45, 49, 52, 54–60, 68, 70, 80, 85, 88–90, 95, 99, 107, 129, 138, 140, 151n3, 153n51

Sankoh, Foday, 31, 33, 35, 39, 140, 151n3

Secret societies, 24–25, 79, 151n7

Securitization, 7–8, 46, 61, 85–97, 115, 148n22. *See also* Copenhagen School

Security, 39, 71, 93, 100–101, 118–119, 146; and development, 3–5, 10, 14, 16–17, 61, 68, 130, 133–134, 142; and the domestic sphere, 6–9, 14, 46–51, 62, 104, 111–112, 115

Security flashes, 8, 10, 16, 112, 115

Sesay, Sulay, 40, 74, 90–91, 110, 155n88, 155n1, 159n16, 160n40, 160n48, 161n5, 165n55

Sexuality: Foucault and, 11, 149n36; gender and, 8; regulation of, 4, 23, 27, 115, 119; representations of African, 28

Sexual slavery, 40, 42, 46, 49, 52, 56–61, 87, 93, 106, 108, 112–113, 125, 144. *See also* Forced marriage

Sexual violence, 32; as a tactic of war, 40; security impacts of, 100–102. *See also* Rape

Shiaka, Dehunge, 107, 120, 124, 128, 133, 153n40, 159n16, 166n9, 166n11, 167n19, 167n25, 168n42

Sierra Leone, civil war, 2–3, 23, 30–38; colonization and, 25–30; gender norms and, 4–5, 24–25, 46–48; government of, 37; history, 23–43. *See also* Sierra Leone Army; Special Court of Sierra Leone

Sierra Leone Army, 18, 31–32, 37–38, 41, 70, 81, 112

Smillie, Ian, 151n3, 151n4

Smith, Malinda, 147n2

Social norms: construction of, 4, 10, 119, 122; as gendered, 101, 115, 142; lack thereof, 51

Social order: construction of, 4; gendered, 15, 49, 64; liberal version of, 12, 83; and peace, 3, 65

Soldier: construction of, 15, 46, 138; definition of, 53, 45–62, 87; and "non-soldiers," 48; representations of, 1–2, 147n1. *See also* Child soldiers; Female soldiers

South Africa, and Executive Outcomes, 32, 94

Special Court of Sierra Leone, 20, 112–113, 165n61, 166n65, 166n67

Spitzer, Leo, 27

Spivak, Gayatri Chakravorty, 10, 149n34

Stevens, Jacqueline, 10–13, 17, 65, 73, 100, 104, 119, 132, 149n47, 150n53, 156n7, 158n5, 160n46, 162n2, 164n25, 166n5, 168n38

Strasser, Captain Valentine, 32–33,

Sylvester, Christine, 9, 65, 145, 148n24, 148n26, 148n27, 149n32

Talking Drum Studio, 90, 162n15

Taylor, Charles, 30, 31, 33, 112

Truth and Reconciliation Commission, 20, 37, 40, 106, 112, 164n32

United Nations, 15, 18, 62, 64, 112, 151n6, 155n100, 158n11, 160n38; Development Program, 67, 105, 110; Human Development Index, 23, 67; Mission in Sierra Leone, 32, 36–37, 39, 68–69, 140; Observer Mission in Sierra Leone, 35, 69; Population Fund, 67

United Nations' International Children's Emergency Fund (UNICEF), 18, 72, 77, 86–87, 103, 157n41, 164n22; Girls Left Behind program, 42, 72, 154n82; UNICEF Sierra Leone, 56, 75, 123, 128, 133

United Nations' Population Fund (UNFPA), 67

United States Agency for International Development (USAID), 71, 160n31

Victim: ideal, 47–50, 86–87; perpetrator dichotomy, 8–9, 15–16, 47–50, 55, 62, 97, 138, 144–145

War babies, 22, 81, 118, 123–135; international community and, 132–133; peacekeepers and, 124–135; stigmatization and, 125–132

Women: as abductees, 42, 107; construction as victims, 46–50, 62, 74, 86–87; contributions to warfare, 40, 47–48, 51–55, 62, 156n6; leaders, 42, 94; as naturally peaceful, 45–48, 62, 117–119; as refugees or displaced people, 107–108; regulation of, 28, 141; as a security concern, 50–51, 61–62, 133–134, 144–146; violence against, 46, 106–112, 156n8; women and children as coherent category, 42, 48. *See also* Disarmament, Demobilization and Reintegration, empowerment and

World Bank, Multi-Donor Trust Fund, 37

World Food Program, 35

Zimbabwe, and Exectuive Outcomes, 32

ABOUT THE AUTHOR

Megan H. MacKenzie is a lecturer in the Department of Government and International Relations at the University of Sydney and a faculty affiliate with the Women and Public Policy Program at Harvard University.